WEIGHT WATCHERS®

1985

ENGAGEMENT CALENDAR

A PLUME BOOK

NEW AMERICAN LIBRARY

NEW YORK AND SCARBOROUGH, ONTARIO

PLUME TRADEMARK REG. U.S. PAT. OFF. AND FOREIGN COUNTRIES
REG. TRADEMARK—MARCA REGISTRADA

SIGNET, SIGNET CLASSIC, MENTOR, PLUME, MERIDIAN and NAL BOOKS
are published *in the United States* by New American Library,
1633 Broadway, New York, New York 10019, *in Canada* by
The New American Library of Canada Limited, 81 Mack Avenue,
Scarborough, Ontario M1L 1M8

LIBRARY OF CONGRESS CATALOGING IN PUBLICATION DATA
Main entry under title:
Weight Watchers 1985 engagement calendar.
    1. Reducing diets.   2. Calendars.   I. Weight Watchers
International.
RM222.2.W2995   1984   613.2'5   83-24420
ISBN 0-452-25500-7 (pbk.)

Designed by John Lynch

Cover painting
Severin Roesen *Still Life with Fruit* © Sotheby Parke-Bernet/Art Resource

Weight Watchers and are registered trademarks of
Weight Watchers International, Inc.

First Printing, August, 1984

     3   4   5   6   7   8   9

PRINTED IN THE UNITED STATES OF AMERICA

WEIGHT WATCHERS 1985 ENGAGEMENT CALENDAR does more than just let you keep track of your weekly appointments; it offers special features to help make a weight-loss regimen successful and enjoyable. Each week of the year has a special recipe, prepared and tested by the Weight Watchers kitchen, with a menu plan that incorporates that recipe, plus helpful tips on cooking and shopping and suggestions on ways to vary the featured dish by substituting other ingredients you might have on hand (for example, using turkey, veal, or ham in a recipe that calls for chicken). A section at the back offers ideas for balanced take-along lunches for school or office as well as suggestions for sensible "lunches out."

The Food Diary page enables the user to keep a record of weekly food intake, for Weight Watchers members know that you have to be aware of what and how much you are eating in order to attain and maintain the right weight for you.

Finally, the weekly message from Weight Watchers founder Jean Nidetch offers time-tested, positive tips on avoiding the pitfalls that can confront the dieter as well as giving the kind of warm, supportive encouragement that has made the Weight Watchers Organization unique.

Over two decades have passed since Jean Nidetch first banded together with six friends in a group effort to stay on a safe, balanced, nutritious diet. That comradeship and mutual support have grown with the years and now reach round the globe. Today Weight Watchers is the largest weight-loss organization in the world. No matter where you are, a Weight Watchers group is nearby; use the telephone directory at the back of this book to locate groups in the U.S. and Canada.

It is our hope that this book will help make the year 1985 a happy and successful one for you.

Cheese Log

Baked Flounder Fillet Roll-Up

Broccoli Spears with Lemon

Lettuce Wedge with Herb Vinaigrette

Half Pink Grapefruit Sprinkled
with Cinnamon

Champagne

HELPFUL HINTS: *To vary the Cheese Log recipe,* use shredded Gouda, Monterey Jack, domestic Swiss, or provolone instead of Cheddar.

For school or office lunch, pack slices of Cheese Log with melba rounds, some crisp raw vegetables, and fresh fruit.

Time-saving tips: Keep shredded cheese on hand in a plastic container in the refrigerator to save time in making this recipe as well as others. To make mincing parsley easier and faster, towel-dry it before cutting.

A WORD FROM JEAN NIDETCH: Ring out the old you, and ring in the new with a savvy tip: Never walk into a party feeling famished. It's easier to cope with an endless array of food if you fortify yourself ahead of time with one or two nutritious, figure-saving snacks, like a fruit or a salad. Fortify your *thinking,* too, by keeping in mind that the fun doesn't have to be the food. Learn to feast on the decorations, the music, and the camaraderie.

PLAN FOR SUCCESS

What I succeeded at this week _____

_____

Goal for next week _____

Cheese Log

Makes 8 servings

A wonderful hors d'oeuvre or appetizer for your New Year's Eve celebration. It can be prepared a day in advance and refrigerated.

4 ounces sharp Cheddar cheese, shredded
⅓ cup part-skim ricotta cheese
1 tablespoon plus 1 teaspoon dry white wine
⅛ teaspoon each garlic powder and onion salt
¼ cup minced fresh parsley
24 melba rounds

In blender container combine cheeses, wine, garlic powder, and onion salt; process at low speed until smooth (using a rubber scraper, scrape down sides of container as necessary).

Onto center of sheet of plastic wrap sprinkle 2 tablespoons parsley; spoon cheese mixture over parsley in a 5-inch-long line. Sprinkle remaining 2 tablespoons parsley over cheese; enclose cheese in wrap, forming a log about 6 inches long x 2 inches wide. Transfer to freezer and let freeze for about 20 minutes; turn log over and freeze until firm, 10 to 25 minutes longer.

To serve, remove plastic wrap and center log on serving platter; surround with melba rounds.

Each serving provides: ½ Protein Exchange; ½ Bread Exchange; 25 calories Optional Exchange
Per serving: 111 calories, 6 g protein, 6 g fat, 8 g carbohydrate, 128 mg sodium, 18 mg cholesterol

WEEKLY FOOD DIARY

		MONDAY	TUESDAY	WEDNESDAY	THURSDAY	FRIDAY	SATURDAY	SUNDAY
BREAKFAST	FRUIT							½ grapefruit
	PROTEIN						2 eggs – Bacon	1 cereal
	BREAD						½ mp	
	FAT							
	MILK						½ mp	1 c
	OPTIONAL							30 c
LUNCH	PROTEIN							Roast ground
	BREAD							noodle
	VEGETABLES							cauliflower
	FAT						cake	1 fat
	FRUIT							½ c tomato juice
	MILK							1 c milk ¼ mp apple
	OPTIONAL							3 lsp flr 30 c
DINNER	PROTEIN						3 ham	30 3 ham
	BREAD							noodle
	VEGETABLES						3 veg ½ c	cauliflower
	FAT						1 fat 30 g	
	FRUIT							½ c mp pineapple
	MILK							
	OPTIONAL						10 c m	
SNACKS								

DAILY CHECK LIST	MONDAY	TUESDAY	WEDNESDAY	THURSDAY	FRIDAY	SATURDAY	SUNDAY
FRUIT	○○○○○	○○○○○	○○○○○	○○○○○	○○○○○	○○○○○	⊗⊗⊗⊗○
VEG.	○○○○	○○○○	○○○○	○○○○	○○○○	○○○○	⊗⊗⊗⊗
MILK	○○○○	○○○○	○○○○	○○○○	○○○○	○○○○	⊗⊗⊗⊗
BREAD	○○○○	○○○○	○○○○	○○○○	○○○○	○○○○	⊗⊗⊗⊗
FAT	○○○○	○○○○	○○○○	○○○○	○○○○	○○○○	⊗⊗⊗⊗
PROTEIN	○○○○	○○○○	○○○○	○○○○	○○○○	○○○○	⊗⊗⊗⊗
OPTIONAL CALORIES	☐	☐	☐	☐	☐	☐	50

WEEKLY CHECKLIST OF LIMITED PROTEIN EXCHANGES

EGGS ○○○	MEAT GROUP ○○○○○○○○○○	
SEMISOFT OR HARD CHEESE ○○○	LIVER ○○○○	

COMMENTS:

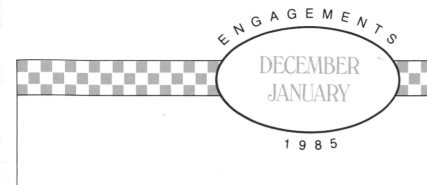

MONDAY
31

New Year's Day   1985

TUESDAY
1

WEDNESDAY
2

THURSDAY
3

FRIDAY
4

SATURDAY
5

SUNDAY
6

	S	M	T	W	T	F	S
							1
D	2	3	4	5	6	7	8
E	9	10	11	12	13	14	15
C	16	17	18	19	20	21	22
	23	24	25	26	27	28	29
	30	31					

	S	M	T	W	T	F	S
			1	2	3	4	5
J	6	7	8	9	10	11	12
A	13	14	15	16	17	18	19
N	20	21	22	23	24	25	26
	27	28	29	30	31		

	S	M	T	W	T	F	S
						1	2
F	3	4	5	6	7	8	9
E	10	11	12	13	14	15	16
B	17	18	19	20	21	22	23
	24	25	26	27	28		

Tomato Juice with Lemon Wedge

Turkey Tetrazzini

Steamed Zucchini Slices

Tossed Salad with Reduced-Calorie
Italian Dressing

Pear Slices Sprinkled with Nutmeg

Coffee or Tea

HELPFUL HINTS: *For economy's sake,* use reconstituted nonfat dry milk instead of skim milk in this week's recipe, and in other casseroles, too. You can't taste the difference, but your purse will feel it.

For an interesting variation, substitute leftover shredded chicken or ham instead of the turkey. And try using leftover cooked pasta and vegetables such as carrots or green beans to make Turkey Tetrazzini.

A WORD FROM JEAN NIDETCH: Make this your year to don a pair of success-colored glasses. Instead of concentrating on your failures, zero in on your accomplishments, no matter how small they may seem. Give yourself a pat on the back every time you do well. (The hand that's patting is too busy to be rummaging in the refrigerator!) Our weekly *Plan for Success* (below) will help feed that "can do" feeling. Fill it in each week and reread the pages for a motivational boost on difficult days.

PLAN FOR SUCCESS

What I succeeded at this week _____

_____

Goal for next week _____

Turkey Tetrazzini

Makes 2 servings

2 teaspoons margarine
½ cup each diced onion and sliced mushrooms
½ garlic clove, minced
1 teaspoon all-purpose flour
1 packet instant chicken broth and seasoning mix
1 cup skim milk
6 ounces skinned and boned cooked turkey, shredded
1 cup cooked spinach macaroni shells
¼ cup chopped drained canned pimientos
2 ounces grated Parmesan or Romano cheese, divided

In small skillet heat margarine until bubbly and hot; add onion, mushrooms, and garlic and sauté, stirring occasionally, until vegetables are soft. Combine flour and broth mix and sprinkle over vegetables; stir to combine and cook for 1 minute. Gradually stir in milk and, stirring constantly, bring to a boil. Reduce heat and cook, stirring, until mixture thickens, about 1 minute; remove from heat and set aside.

Preheat oven to 375°F. Spray a 1-quart casserole with nonstick cooking spray. Combine turkey, macaroni, pimientos, and 1 ounce cheese in casserole and pour vegetable sauce over mixture; sprinkle with remaining 1 ounce cheese and bake until thoroughly heated, about 30 minutes. If crisper topping is desired, turn oven control to broil and broil tetrazzini for 1 minute (be sure to use a flameproof casserole).

Each serving provides: 4 Protein Exchanges; 1 Bread Exchange; 1¼ Vegetable Exchanges; 1 Fat Exchange; ½ Milk Exchange; 10 calories Optional Exchange

Per serving: 470 calories, 46 g protein, 18 g fat, 30 g carbohydrate, 1,130 mg sodium, 110 mg cholesterol

WEEKLY FOOD DIARY

	MONDAY	TUESDAY	WEDNESDAY	THURSDAY	FRIDAY	SATURDAY	SUNDAY
BREAKFAST FRUIT	½ grapefruit	½ grapefruit	½ grapefruit	½ grapefruit	½ grapefruit	½ fruit	½ fruit
PROTEIN	cereal	1 egg	1 egg	cereal	cereal		
BREAD							
FAT							
MILK	1 c	1 c	1 c	1 c	1 c	1 c	1 c
OPTIONAL							
LUNCH PROTEIN		3 ham	3 ham	3 ham	2 ham		
BREAD		cheese	1 cheese	1 cheese	1 cheese		
VEGETABLES							
FAT							
FRUIT	applesauce	applesauce	applesauce	applesauce			
MILK	1 c	1 c	1 c				
OPTIONAL							
DINNER PROTEIN			steak 3	steak 3	steak 3	steak 4	
BREAD							
VEGETABLES		salad	salad + 1	salad + 1	salad + 1		
FAT	dressing	dressing	dressing	dressing	dressing		
FRUIT	applesauce	applesauce	applesauce				
MILK	1 c	1 c				30 oz	
OPTIONAL	1 hot choco			1 pc choco			
SNACKS	graham crackers	graham crackers	graham cracker				
DAILY CHECK LIST							
FRUIT							
VEG.							
MILK							
BREAD							
FAT							
PROTEIN							
OPTIONAL							
CALORIES		30	30				

WEEKLY CHECKLIST OF LIMITED PROTEIN EXCHANGES

EGGS ○○○○○○

MEAT GROUP ○○○○○○○○○○

SEMISOFT OR HARD CHEESE ○○○○○○

LIVER ○○○○

COMMENTS:

MONDAY
7

Lemony Sole Meuniere Sept 16

TUESDAY
8

WEDNESDAY
9

Beef Kabobs Jelly 1

THURSDAY
10

FRIDAY
11

SATURDAY
12

SUNDAY
13

	S	M	T	W	T	F	S
D							1
E	2	3	4	5	6	7	8
C	9	10	11	12	13	14	15
	16	17	18	19	20	21	22
	23	24	25	26	27	28	29
	30	31					

	S	M	T	W	T	F	S
			1	2	3	4	5
J	6	7	8	9	10	11	12
A	13	14	15	16	17	18	19
N	20	21	22	23	24	25	26
	27	28	29	30	31		

	S	M	T	W	T	F	S
						1	2
F	3	4	5	6	7	8	9
E	10	11	12	13	14	15	16
B	17	18	19	20	21	22	23
	24	25	26	27	28		

Fennel Soup

Roast Chicken over Noodles

Steamed Brussels Sprouts with Sesame Seed

Orange Sections Sprinkled
with Shredded Coconut

Cinnamon Coffee or Herbal Tea

HELPFUL HINTS: *For added flavor,* sprinkle Fennel Soup with grated Parmesan cheese.

For future use, freeze soup in serving-sized portions for a speedy thaw-and-heat dish.

Leftover fresh fennel can be sliced and added to a tossed salad, used braised or breaded and sautéed as a vegetable, or added to stews and other soups for flavoring.

A WORD FROM JEAN NIDETCH: On cooped-up wintry days, the hum of the refrigerator may seem like your song. Tune it out by surrounding yourself with *non*edible interests. Have them accessible at a moment's notice—an opened book in the bedroom, a record album in plain view in the living room. If your hobby is painting, have the easel or oils set out. If you yearn to write, leave the typewriter out of its case. Make certain that your knitting, needlepoint, stamp album—whatever—are all within easier reach than food. House-bound doesn't have to mean kitchen-bound!

PLAN FOR SUCCESS

What I succeeded at this week _____

_____

Goal for next week _____

Fennel Soup

Makes 2 servings

Fennel, a flavorful vegetable that looks like a member of the celery family, has an unusual taste reminiscent of licorice.

2 teaspoons unsalted margarine
2 cups diced fennel
½ cup diced carrot
¼ cup each diced onion and celery
1½ packets (1½ teaspoons) instant
     chicken broth and seasoning mix
1 cup water

In 1-quart saucepan melt margarine; add vegetables and broth mix and stir until vegetables are coated with margarine. Add water and bring to a boil. Reduce heat, cover pan, and let simmer until vegetables are tender, 20 to 25 minutes.

Pour half of soup mixture into blender container and process until smooth; return pureed mixture to saucepan and stir to combine.

Each serving provides: 3 Vegetable Exchanges; 1 Fat Exchange; 10 calories Optional Exchange
Per serving: 96 calories, 4 g protein, 4 g fat, 12 g carbohydrate, 861 mg sodium, 0 mg cholesterol

WEEKLY FOOD DIARY

	MONDAY	TUESDAY	WEDNESDAY	THURSDAY	FRIDAY	SATURDAY	SUNDAY
BREAKFAST FRUIT PROTEIN BREAD FAT MILK OPTIONAL							
LUNCH PROTEIN BREAD VEGETABLES FAT FRUIT MILK OPTIONAL							
DINNER PROTEIN BREAD VEGETABLES FAT FRUIT MILK OPTIONAL							
SNACKS							
DAILY CHECK LIST FRUIT VEG. MILK BREAD FAT PROTEIN OPTIONAL	CALORIES	CALORIES	CALORIES	CALORIES	CALORIES	CALORIES	CALORIES

WEEKLY CHECKLIST OF LIMITED PROTEIN EXCHANGES

EGGS ○○○○

MEAT GROUP ○○○○○○○○○○

SEMISOFT OR HARD CHEESE ○○○○

LIVER ○○○○○○

COMMENTS:

MONDAY
14

Martin Luther King, Jr.'s Birthday

TUESDAY
15

WEDNESDAY
16

THURSDAY
17

FRIDAY
18

SATURDAY
19

SUNDAY
20

	S	M	T	W	T	F	S
D E C							1
	2	3	4	5	6	7	8
	9	10	11	12	13	14	15
	16	17	18	19	20	21	22
	23	24	25	26	27	28	29
	30	31					

	S	M	T	W	T	F	S
J A N			1	2	3	4	5
	6	7	8	9	10	11	12
	13	14	15	16	17	18	19
	20	21	22	23	24	25	26
	27	28	29	30	31		

	S	M	T	W	T	F	S
F E B						1	2
	3	4	5	6	7	8	9
	10	11	12	13	14	15	16
	17	18	19	20	21	22	23
	24	25	26	27	28		

WEIGHT

MENU

WATCHERS

Chicken Consommé

Vegetable-Cheese Puff

French Bread

Green Bell Pepper Rings and
Tomato Slices

Baked Apple with Cinnamon and
Whipped Topping

Coffee or Tea

HELPFUL HINTS: *To vary this week's recipe,* use well-drained, cooked chopped spinach, asparagus, broccoli, or sliced zucchini instead of the cauliflower and carrots.

For a delicious side dish, simply follow first step of the recipe and presto!—sautéed vegetables.

The secret to beating egg whites? (1) Use an absolutely clean, dry bowl and beaters. (2) Beat the whites right before you are ready to use them. The consistency is right when you can turn the bowl upside down and they cling to the bowl and don't slide.

A WORD FROM JEAN NIDETCH: Some people nibble on food when what they really want to do is chew someone out. Try feasting on some assertiveness instead. You don't have to hit the other person over the head, just *assert* your right to have your needs and feelings respected. Be direct in saying what you want or how you feel. Even if it doesn't always solve the problem, *expressing* your feelings is more effective than *swallowing* them (along with too much food)!

PLAN FOR SUCCESS

What I succeeded at this week _____

_____

Goal for next week _____

Vegetable-Cheese Puff

Makes 4 servings

2 tablespoons plus 2 teaspoons margarine, divided
1 teaspoon minced fresh garlic
2 cups each cooked chopped cauliflower and cooked
    sliced carrots
½ teaspoon salt
1½ cups part-skim ricotta cheese
4 eggs, separated (at room temperature)
2 tablespoons chopped fresh parsley
1 tablespoon plus 1 teaspoon grated Romano cheese
¼ teaspoon pepper

In 10-inch nonstick skillet that has a metal or removable handle heat 1 tablespoon plus 1 teaspoon margarine over medium heat until bubbly and hot; add garlic and sauté for about 30 seconds (*do not brown*). Add vegetables and salt and sauté for 3 minutes. Remove vegetable mixture to a plate and wipe skillet clean; set aside.

Preheat oven to 400°F. In large mixing bowl combine ricotta cheese, egg yolks, parsley, Romano cheese, and pepper; using electric mixer, beat until smooth.

In separate bowl, using clean beaters, beat egg whites until stiff peaks form; fold beaten whites alternately with vegetable mixture into cheese mixture.

In same skillet heat remaining margarine until bubbly and hot; add cheese mixture and, using spatula, gently smooth surface. Transfer skillet to upper-third portion of oven and bake for 15 minutes (until puffy and browned); serve immediately.

Each serving provides: 2½ Protein Exchanges; 2 Vegetable Exchanges; 2 Fat Exchanges; 10 calories Optional Exchange
Per serving: 320 calories, 20 g protein, 21 g fat, 14 g carbohydrate, 593 mg sodium, 305 mg cholesterol

WEEKLY FOOD DIARY

	MONDAY	TUESDAY	WEDNESDAY	THURSDAY	FRIDAY	SATURDAY	SUNDAY
BREAKFAST FRUIT PROTEIN BREAD FAT MILK OPTIONAL							
LUNCH PROTEIN BREAD VEGETABLES FAT FRUIT MILK OPTIONAL							
DINNER PROTEIN BREAD VEGETABLES FAT FRUIT MILK OPTIONAL							
SNACKS							

DAILY CHECK LIST

FRUIT
VEG.
MILK
BREAD
FAT
PROTEIN
OPTIONAL

CALORIES (per day)

WEEKLY CHECKLIST OF LIMITED PROTEIN EXCHANGES

EGGS ○○○○ ○○

MEAT GROUP ○○○○○○○○○○

SEMISOFT OR HARD CHEESE ○○○ ○○

LIVER ○○○

COMMENTS:

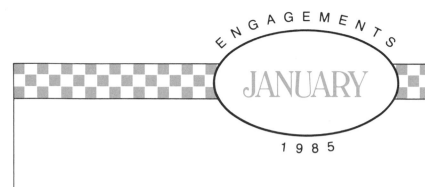

MONDAY
21

TUESDAY
22

WEDNESDAY
23

THURSDAY
24

FRIDAY
25

SATURDAY
26

SUNDAY
27

	S	M	T	W	T	F	S
							1
D	2	3	4	5	6	7	8
E	9	10	11	12	13	14	15
C	16	17	18	19	20	21	22
	23	24	25	26	27	28	29
	30	31					

	S	M	T	W	T	F	S
			1	2	3	4	5
J	6	7	8	9	10	11	12
A	13	14	15	16	17	18	19
N	20	21	22	23	24	25	26
	27	28	29	30	31		

	S	M	T	W	T	F	S
						1	2
F	3	4	5	6	7	8	9
E	10	11	12	13	14	15	16
B	17	18	19	20	21	22	23
	24	25	26	27	28		

Baked Ham

Glazed Baby Carrots

Steamed Cauliflower Florets

Sliced Tomato and Cucumber on Lettuce
Sprinkled with Oil and Vinegar

Apple Strudel

Coffee or Tea

HELPFUL HINTS: *Vary the recipe* by using 5 small pears instead of apples. Out of allspice? Try cinnamon or nutmeg instead.

As a spinoff, use the Apple Strudel filling as you would applesauce. This filling can also be frozen and kept on hand for baking later in the month.

Two kitchen tricks: Want lump-free confectioners' sugar? Try sifting it through a tea strainer. Keep pared, cut apples from darkening by brushing with lemon juice. Better yet, don't prepare them until just before you are ready to use them.

A WORD FROM JEAN NIDETCH: Seldom hear an encouraging word? Set up a "hot line" with friends who are trying to control their weight. Phone each other when you need a quick boost. Call when you do well, too, so you can feast on some positive reinforcement. Don't forget to pass along tasty new recipes (like the ones here and in the Weight Watchers cookbooks) or your own trimmed-down versions of fattening favorites.

PLAN FOR SUCCESS

What I succeeded at this week _____

_____

Goal for next week _____

Apple Strudel

Makes 10 servings

This is a recipe that can be prepared, baked, and frozen. Thaw and serve for a quick dessert when company comes.

> 5 small Granny Smith apples, cored, pared, and
>   thinly sliced
> 1 tablespoon plus 2 teaspoons granulated sugar
> 1 tablespoon lemon juice
> ⅛ teaspoon ground allspice
> 1 package (10 ounces) refrigerated buttermilk
>   flaky biscuits (10 biscuits)
> 1 tablespoon confectioners' sugar

In 1-quart saucepan combine first 4 ingredients; bring mixture to a boil. Reduce heat to low, cover pan, and let simmer until apples are soft; remove from heat and let cool.

Separate biscuits. On sheet of wax paper place biscuits next to each other, two by two, forming a rectangle; press edges of biscuits together to seal. Cover with another sheet of wax paper and, using a rolling pin, roll dough into a thin rectangle, about 15 × 8 inches.

Preheat oven to 400°F. Spoon cooled apple mixture down center of dough; moisten edges of dough with water and fold ends in and sides over to enclose filling, pinching edges together to seal.

Spray a nonstick baking sheet with nonstick cooking spray; using a large spatula, gently lift strudel onto baking sheet. Bake until golden brown, 12 to 15 minutes (if strudel is browning too rapidly, cover with foil).

Transfer strudel to wire rack and let cool completely; sift confectioners' sugar over entire surface of strudel. To serve, slice into 10 equal pieces.

Each serving provides: 1 Bread Exchange; ½ Fruit Exchange; 15 calories Optional Exchange

Per serving: 118 calories, 2 g protein, 2 g fat, 23 g carbohydrate, 246 mg sodium, 0 mg cholesterol

WEEKLY FOOD DIARY

	MONDAY	TUESDAY	WEDNESDAY	THURSDAY	FRIDAY	SATURDAY	SUNDAY
BREAKFAST FRUIT PROTEIN BREAD FAT MILK OPTIONAL							
LUNCH PROTEIN BREAD VEGETABLES FAT FRUIT MILK OPTIONAL							
DINNER PROTEIN BREAD VEGETABLES FAT FRUIT MILK OPTIONAL							
SNACKS							
DAILY CHECK LIST FRUIT VEG. MILK BREAD FAT PROTEIN OPTIONAL	○○○ ○○○ ○○○ ○○○ ○○○ ○○○○○○○ □ CALORIES	○ ○○○ ○○○ ○○○ ○○○ ○○○○○○○ □ CALORIES	○○○ ○○○ ○○○ ○○○ ○○○ ○○○○○○○ □ CALORIES	○○○ ○○○ ○○○ ○○○ ○○○ ○○○○○○○ □ CALORIES	○○○ ○○○ ○○○ ○○○ ○○○ ○○○○○○○ □ CALORIES	○○○ ○○○ ○○○ ○○○ ○○○○○○○ □ CALORIES	○○○ ○○○ ○○○ ○○○ ○○○ ○○○○○○○ □ CALORIES

WEEKLY CHECKLIST OF LIMITED PROTEIN EXCHANGES

EGGS ○○○○	MEAT GROUP ○○○○○○○○○○○	
SEMISOFT OR HARD CHEESE ○○○○	LIVER ○○○○○○	

COMMENTS:

JANUARY
FEBRUARY

1 9 8 5

MONDAY
28

TUESDAY
29

WEDNESDAY
30

THURSDAY
31

FRIDAY
1

SATURDAY
2

SUNDAY
3

	S	M	T	W	T	F	S
D							1
E	2	3	4	5	6	7	8
C	9	10	11	12	13	14	15
	16	17	18	19	20	21	22
	23	24	25	26	27	28	29
	30	31					

	S	M	T	W	T	F	S
J			1	2	3	4	5
A	6	7	8	9	10	11	12
N	13	14	15	16	17	18	19
	20	21	22	23	24	25	26
	27	28	29	30	31		

	S	M	T	W	T	F	S
F						1	2
E	3	4	5	6	7	8	9
B	10	11	12	13	14	15	16
	17	18	19	20	21	22	23
	24	25	26	27	28		

Savory Pot Roast

Parslied Boiled Potatoes

Mixed Green Salad with
Italian Dressing

Baked Pear Sprinkled
with Cinnamon

Coffee or Tea

HELPFUL HINTS: *Budget-stretching* pot roasts use less tender economy cuts that become more flavorful the longer they cook as well as when they are reheated. Leftover pot roast can be turned into a hearty lunchbox sandwich; reheated, it can be served as a hot open-faced sandwich.

As a time-saver, prepare Savory Pot Roast on a day when you're stuck indoors. Once cooked, let it cool slightly, and after removing cloves and bay leaf, store in a covered bowl for up to 5 days. Just reheat for a quick meal on a busy day.

A WORD FROM JEAN NIDETCH: Winter doldrums got you down? Beat February fretfulness with exercise. It's a great antidote to tension and, as a surprising bonus, it also tends to trim feelings of hunger. If bad weather keeps you at home, do some indoor exercising, like climbing up and down the stairs. You'll find your mood climbing, too, while your weight is more likely to go down.

PLAN FOR SUCCESS

What I succeeded at this week _____

_____

Goal for next week _____

Savory Pot Roast

Makes 8 servings

2½-pound boneless beef rump roast (rolled)
1 tablespoon plus 1 teaspoon vegetable oil
2 cups sliced onions
1 large celery rib, cut into 1-inch pieces
1 garlic clove, sliced
4 medium carrots (3 to 4 ounces each), cut
    into 1-inch pieces
3 cups water
¼ cup tomato puree
4 packets instant beef broth and seasoning mix
2 whole cloves
1 bay leaf
Dash each thyme leaves, salt, and pepper
2 tablespoons plus 2 teaspoons all-purpose flour

On rack in roasting pan roast beef at 325°F. until rare, about 45 minutes; remove from oven and set aside.

In 3-quart saucepan heat oil over medium heat; add onions, celery, and garlic and sauté briefly (*do not brown*). Add meat and remaining ingredients except flour; bring liquid to a boil and stir. Reduce heat to low, cover, and let simmer until meat is fork-tender, 2 to 2½ hours.

Remove meat from pan and let stand for 10 minutes; slice meat against the grain. Arrange on serving platter and keep warm. Remove cloves and bay leaf from vegetable mixture; transfer mixture to blender container, add flour, and process until smooth. Return to saucepan and cook until heated and thickened; serve over pot roast.

Each serving provides: 4 Protein Exchanges; 1¾ Vegetable Exchanges; ½ Fat Exchange; 15 calories Optional Exchange

Per serving: 313 calories, 35 g protein, 13 g fat, 12 g carbohydrate, 535 mg sodium, 103 mg cholesterol

WEEKLY FOOD DIARY

DAILY CHECK LIST		MONDAY	TUESDAY	WEDNESDAY	THURSDAY	FRIDAY	SATURDAY	SUNDAY
BREAKFAST	FRUIT PROTEIN BREAD FAT MILK OPTIONAL							Milk
LUNCH	PROTEIN BREAD VEGETABLES FAT FRUIT MILK OPTIONAL							Pizza 10 cal Pineapple candy
DINNER	PROTEIN BREAD VEGETABLES FAT FRUIT MILK OPTIONAL							steak broccoli, cauliflower Pineapple slices
SNACKS								
	FRUIT VEG. MILK BREAD FAT PROTEIN OPTIONAL	○○○○○○○○ CALORIES	○○○○○○○○ CALORIES	○○○○○○○○ CALORIES	○○○○○○○○ CALORIES	○○○○○○○○ CALORIES	○○○○○○○○ CALORIES	○○○○○○○○ CALORIES

WEEKLY CHECKLIST OF LIMITED PROTEIN EXCHANGES

EGGS ○○○○○○○○

SEMISOFT OR HARD CHEESE ○○○○○○○○

MEAT GROUP ○○○○○○○○○○○○○○

LIVER ○○○○○○○○

COMMENTS:

FEBRUARY

1 9 8 5

MONDAY

4

TUESDAY

5

WEDNESDAY

6

THURSDAY

7

FRIDAY

8

SATURDAY

9

SUNDAY

10

	S	M	T	W	T	F	S
			1	2	3	4	5
J	6	7	8	9	10	11	12
A	13	14	15	16	17	18	19
N	20	21	22	23	24	25	26
	27	28	29	30	31		

	S	M	T	W	T	F	S
						1	2
F	3	4	5	6	7	8	9
E	10	11	12	13	14	15	16
B	17	18	19	20	21	22	23
	24	25	26	27	28		

	S	M	T	W	T	F	S
						1	2
M	3	4	5	6	7	8	9
A	10	11	12	13	14	15	16
R	17	18	19	20	21	22	23
	24	25	26	27	28	29	30
	31						

Chicken Consommé

Tuna Casserole au Gratin

Tomato and Green Bell Pepper Slices
on Lettuce with Tarragon Vinaigrette

Sliced Peaches with Plain Low-Fat Yogurt

Coffee or Tea

HELPFUL HINTS: *Vary this week's recipe* by (1) substituting 1 cup cooked broc-coli florets or cut green beans for the cauliflower; (2) using 8 ounces drained canned salmon instead of the tuna; (3) substituting ¾ cup cooked noodles for the peas.

To transform simple leftovers or low-cost ingredients into a delicious dish, use the cheese sauce with leftover chicken, turkey, ham, or cooked vegetables.

Try these time-savers: Prepare the recipe's main vegetables a day or two ahead of time and refrigerate them. Double the recipe; serve one casserole for dinner and freeze the other for future use.

A WORD FROM JEAN NIDETCH: Does Valentine's Day pose a threat to the view in your mirror? It doesn't have to. Just ask your loved ones to have a heart and gift you with tokens that don't come in candy boxes. Cue them to calorie-less flowers, plants, books, records—even attire that cannily calls attention to your slimming shape.

PLAN FOR SUCCESS

What I succeeded at this week _____

_____

Goal for next week _____

Tuna Casserole au Gratin

Makes 2 servings

8 ounces drained canned tuna, flaked
1 cup cooked cauliflower, chopped
1 cup cooked diced carrots
2 teaspoons margarine
2 tablespoons diced onion
1 tablespoon plus 1½ teaspoons
    all-purpose flour
1 cup skim milk
Dash each salt and pepper
¾ cup frozen green peas, thawed
3 tablespoons shredded Cheddar cheese

In 2-quart casserole combine tuna, cauliflower, and carrots; set aside.

In small saucepan heat margarine over medium heat until bubbly and hot; add onion and sauté until softened, about 2 minutes. Add flour and, using wire whisk, combine thoroughly. Gradually stir in milk; add salt and pepper. Reduce heat to low and cook, stirring constantly, until sauce thickens. Add peas and cheese and stir to combine; pour sauce over tuna mixture and bake at 350°F. for 30 minutes.

Each serving provides: 4 Protein Exchanges; 1 Bread Exchange; 2 Vegetable Exchanges; 1 Fat Exchange; ½ Milk Exchange; 45 calories Optional Exchange

Per serving: 464 calories, 42 g protein, 22 g fat, 27 g carbohydrate, 891 mg sodium, 43 mg cholesterol

WEEKLY FOOD DIARY

	MONDAY	TUESDAY	WEDNESDAY	THURSDAY	FRIDAY	SATURDAY	SUNDAY
BREAKFAST FRUIT PROTEIN BREAD FAT MILK OPTIONAL	grapefruit cereal 1 c. ¼ c	grapefruit cereal milk *(4)*	grapefruit cereal milk *(4)*				
LUNCH PROTEIN BREAD VEGETABLES FAT FRUIT MILK OPTIONAL	cheese Roll-(2) Lettuce Tom mayo 2 tsp orange	*(illegible)* needs lettuce tom mayo tsp orange juice	Burrito				
DINNER PROTEIN BREAD VEGETABLES FAT FRUIT MILK OPTIONAL	steak broccoli mashed pineapple lemon cream	steak brownie *(illegible)*					
SNACKS	1 oatmeal	oatmeal					
DAILY CHECK LIST FRUIT VEG. MILK BREAD FAT PROTEIN OPTIONAL	⊗⊗⊗ ⊗○○ ⊗⊗○ ⊗⊗○ ⊗⊗⊗○○○○ ⊗⊗⊗⊗○○○ ☐5 CALORIES	⊗⊗⊗ ⊗○○ ⊗⊗○ ⊗⊗○ ⊗⊗⊗○○○○ ⊗⊗⊗⊗○○○ ☐5 CALORIES	○○○ ○○○ ○○○ ⊗○○ ⊗⊗⊗○○○○ ⊗⊗⊗⊗○○○ ☐ CALORIES	○○○ ○○○ ○○○ ○○○ ○○○○○○○ ○○○○○○○ ☐ CALORIES	○○○ ○○○ ○○○ ○○○ ○○○○○○○ ○○○○○○○ ☐ CALORIES	○○○ ○○○ ○○○ ○○○ ○○○○○○○ ○○○○○○○ ☐ CALORIES	○○○ ○○○ ○○○ ○○○ ○○○○○○○ ○○○○○○○ ☐ CALORIES

WEEKLY CHECKLIST OF LIMITED PROTEIN EXCHANGES

EGGS ○○○○○○

MEAT GROUP ○○○○○○○○○○○

SEMISOFT OR HARD CHEESE ○○○○○

LIVER ○○○○

COMMENTS:

FEBRUARY

1 9 8 5

MONDAY
11

Lincoln's Birthday

TUESDAY
12

WEDNESDAY
13

Valentine's Day

THURSDAY
14

FRIDAY
15

SATURDAY
16

SUNDAY
17

JAN	S	M	T	W	T	F	S
			1	2	3	4	5
	6	7	8	9	10	11	12
	13	14	15	16	17	18	19
	20	21	22	23	24	25	26
	27	28	29	30	31		

FEB	S	M	T	W	T	F	S
						1	2
	3	4	5	6	7	8	9
	10	11	12	13	14	15	16
	17	18	19	20	21	22	23
	24	25	26	27	28		

MAR	S	M	T	W	T	F	S
						1	2
	3	4	5	6	7	8	9
	10	11	12	13	14	15	16
	17	18	19	20	21	22	23
	24	25	26	27	28	29	30
	31						

Ham and Swiss Cheese on Rye Bread with Mustard

Pickle and Tomato Slices on Lettuce

Carrot Sticks

Celery-Fruit Salad with
Caraway-Yogurt Dressing

Tea with Lemon

HELPFUL HINTS: *To vary the recipe,* make some substitutions: ½ teaspoon of poppy seed for the caraway seed; 2 small pears instead of the apples; 40 small grapes (or 24 large ones) for the raisins.

For a taste treat, top fresh banana or tangerine or canned fruit cocktail with Caraway-Yogurt Dressing.

For school or office lunch, pack leftover salad in a plastic container in an insulated bag or lunch box and accompany it with a sandwich and beverage.

A WORD FROM JEAN NIDETCH: "He never told a lie," so history records about George Washington. Unfortunately, this doesn't always hold true for family and friends who tell us we are getting "too thin" when we still have a way to go. They may be apprehensive that a new you won't want the old relationship. Reassure them that you'll want to be as close as ever, or toss off a jaunty "not thin enough for *me,*" but whatever you do, turn a determinedly deaf ear so you don't turn in your dreams.

PLAN FOR SUCCESS

What I succeeded at this week _____

_____

Goal for next week _____

Celery-Fruit Salad with Caraway-Yogurt Dressing

Makes 4 servings

¼ cup plain low-fat yogurt
2 teaspoons white wine vinegar
½ teaspoon each caraway seed,
    salt, and lemon juice
2 cups thinly sliced celery
2 small Golden Delicious apples,
    cored and diced
¼ cup raisins
8 chilled iceberg lettuce leaves

In medium bowl combine yogurt, vinegar, caraway seed, salt, and lemon juice, mixing well; add remaining ingredients except lettuce and toss thoroughly to combine. Cover and refrigerate until ready to serve.

To serve, chill 4 salad plates; arrange 2 lettuce leaves on each chilled plate. Toss salad again and top each portion of lettuce with ¼ of the salad.

Each serving provides: 1½ Vegetable Exchanges; 1 Fruit Exchange; 15 calories Optional Exchange
Per serving: 80 calories, 2 g protein, 0.4 g fat, 19 g carbohydrate, 358 mg sodium, 0.3 mg cholesterol

WEEKLY FOOD DIARY

	MONDAY	TUESDAY	WEDNESDAY	THURSDAY	FRIDAY	SATURDAY	SUNDAY
BREAKFAST FRUIT PROTEIN BREAD FAT MILK OPTIONAL							
LUNCH PROTEIN BREAD VEGETABLES FAT FRUIT MILK OPTIONAL							
DINNER PROTEIN BREAD VEGETABLES FAT FRUIT MILK OPTIONAL							
SNACKS							
DAILY CHECK LIST FRUIT VEG. MILK BREAD FAT PROTEIN OPTIONAL	○○○ ○○○○ ○○○ ○○○ ○○○○○○○ □ CALORIES	○○ ○○○○ ○○○ ○○○○○○○ □ CALORIES	○○ ○○○○ ○○○○ ○○○○○○○ □ CALORIES	○○ ○○○○ ○○○○ ○○○○○○○ □ CALORIES	○○ ○○○ ○○○ ○○○○○○○ □ CALORIES	○○○ ○○○ ○○○○ ○○○○○○○ □ CALORIES	○○○ ○○○ ○○○ ○○○○○○○ □ CALORIES

WEEKLY CHECKLIST OF LIMITED PROTEIN EXCHANGES

EGGS ○○○○

SEMISOFT OR HARD CHEESE ○○○

MEAT GROUP ○○○○○○○○○○○

LIVER ○○○○○○

COMMENTS:

FEBRUARY

1 9 8 5

Washington's Birthday (observed)

MONDAY
18

TUESDAY
19

Ash Wednesday

WEDNESDAY
20

THURSDAY
21

Washington's Birthday

FRIDAY
22

SATURDAY
23

SUNDAY
24

	S	M	T	W	T	F	S
						1	2	3	4	5
JAN	6	7	8	9	10	11	12
	13	14	15	16	17	18	19
	20	21	22	23	24	25	26
	27	28	29	30	31		

	S	M	T	W	T	F	S
						1	2
FEB	3	4	5	6	7	8	9
	10	11	12	13	14	15	16
	17	18	19	20	21	22	23
	24	25	26	27	28		

	S	M	T	W	T	F	S
						1	2
MAR	3	4	5	6	7	8	9
	10	11	12	13	14	15	16
	17	18	19	20	21	22	23
	24	25	26	27	28	29	30
	31						

Tortilla-Bean Broil

Spinach and Mushroom Salad with
Imitation Bacon Bits

Orange and Grapefruit Sections with
Toasted Shredded Coconut

Sparkling Mineral Water with
Lime Twist

HELPFUL HINTS: *An avocado is ripe* when it yields to light pressure on the rind and when a toothpick inserted at the stem end moves in and out freely. *To ripen an avocado,* keep it at room temperature. *To speed up ripening,* place it in an opened paper or plastic bag.

For a fast crouton substitute for salads or soups, use lightly crushed taco shells.

A WORD FROM JEAN NIDETCH: Walk into a restaurant with your mind made up about what you'll order; don't let a glance at the menu sway you from your course. Order crudités or a "safe" appetizer right away to avoid the temptation of bread. Remember that a glass of wine has fewer calories than a cocktail, and when dessert time comes, request fruit. If it isn't on the dessert menu, check out the appetizers, which usually include items like melon. You can prove that dining out doesn't have to mean losing out—figure-atively speaking.

PLAN FOR SUCCESS

What I succeeded at this week _____

_____

Goal for next week _____

Tortilla-Bean Broil

Makes 2 servings

Fiery hot chilies give this dish a truly Mexican flavor, but mild chilies can be substituted.

8 ounces drained canned pink pinto beans
½ cup tomato sauce
1 tablespoon plus 1 teaspoon minced onion
2 teaspoons minced drained canned hot chilies
2 corn tortillas (6-inch diameter each), heated
2 ounces sharp Cheddar cheese, coarsely shredded
¼ avocado (2 ounces), pared and sliced

In blender container combine beans, tomato sauce, onion, and chilies; process until pureed. Break each tortilla into quarters and place into 1-quart flameproof casserole; top with bean mixture and sprinkle with cheese. Broil until cheese is melted, 3 to 5 minutes. Serve garnished with avocado slices.

Each serving provides: 3 Protein Exchanges; 1 Bread Exchange; 1 Vegetable Exchange; 50 calories Optional Exchange

Per serving: 357 calories, 18 g protein, 15 g fat, 41 g carbohydrate, 859 mg sodium (estimated), 30 mg cholesterol

WEEKLY FOOD DIARY

	MONDAY	TUESDAY	WEDNESDAY	THURSDAY	FRIDAY	SATURDAY	SUNDAY
BREAKFAST FRUIT PROTEIN BREAD FAT MILK OPTIONAL							
LUNCH PROTEIN BREAD VEGETABLES FAT FRUIT MILK OPTIONAL							
DINNER PROTEIN BREAD VEGETABLES FAT FRUIT MILK OPTIONAL							
SNACKS							
DAILY CHECK LIST FRUIT VEG. MILK BREAD FAT PROTEIN OPTIONAL	○○○○○○○○○ CALORIES	○○○○○○○○○ CALORIES	○○○○○○○○○ CALORIES	○○○○○○○○○ CALORIES	○○○○○○○○○ CALORIES	○○○○○○○○○ CALORIES	○○○○○○○○○ CALORIES

WEEKLY CHECKLIST OF LIMITED PROTEIN EXCHANGES

EGGS ○○○

SEMISOFT OR HARD CHEESE ○○○

MEAT GROUP ○○○○○○○○○○○○

LIVER ○○○○○○○

COMMENTS:

FEBRUARY
MARCH

1 9 8 5

MONDAY
25

TUESDAY
26

WEDNESDAY
27

THURSDAY
28

FRIDAY
1

SATURDAY
2

SUNDAY
3

	S	M	T	W	T	F	S
JAN			1	2	3	4	5
	6	7	8	9	10	11	12
	13	14	15	16	17	18	19
	20	21	22	23	24	25	26
	27	28	29	30	31		

	S	M	T	W	T	F	S
FEB						1	2
	3	4	5	6	7	8	9
	10	11	12	13	14	15	16
	17	18	19	20	21	22	23
	24	25	26	27	28		

	S	M	T	W	T	F	S
MAR						1	2
	3	4	5	6	7	8	9
	10	11	12	13	14	15	16
	17	18	19	20	21	22	23
	24	25	26	27	28	29	30
	31						

WEIGHT

MENU

WATCHERS

Chicken Croquettes

Steamed Carrot Slices and
Cauliflower Florets

Tossed Salad with Reduced-Calorie
Thousand Island Dressing

Spiced Applesauce

Coffee or Tea

HELPFUL HINTS: *For easier shaping,* spread the croquette mixture in a pan sprayed with nonstick cooking spray, cover, and refrigerate briefly. Once chilled, it can easily be cut and shaped into croquettes.

Make your own bread crumbs by processing stale bread in the blender or processor (use 1 ounce or 1 slice of bread, made into crumbs, in place of 3 tablespoons of crumbs).

To save time, keep labeled, wrapped 3-ounce portions of skinned and boned cooked chicken in the freezer. It will keep for about 2 months, giving you instant crêpes, sandwiches, salads, and, of course, croquettes.

A WORD FROM JEAN NIDETCH: Do you tell yourself you're a "100 percent failure" every time you make a mistake? There's nothing to be gained from that (except weight). For more rewarding arithmetic, you can estimate that there are 10,080 minutes in a week. Think of the high percentage of *successful* moments you had. Then, instead of dismissing your efforts as a zero, aim for a higher percentage next week.

PLAN FOR SUCCESS

What I succeeded at this week _____

_____

Goal for next week _____

Chicken Croquettes

Makes 2 servings, 4 croquettes each

2 tablespoons plus 2 teaspoons reduced-calorie
   margarine, divided
3 tablespoons all-purpose flour, divided
½ cup skim milk (at room temperature)
6 ounces skinned and boned cooked chicken, ground
1 packet instant chicken broth and seasoning mix
3 tablespoons plain dried bread crumbs
1 egg, lightly beaten

In small saucepan heat 1 tablespoon margarine over medium heat until bubbly and hot; add 1 tablespoon plus 1 teaspoon flour and cook, stirring constantly, for 1 minute. Continuing to stir, gradually add milk and bring to a boil. Reduce heat to low and cook, stirring, until mixture is thickened and smooth; stir in chicken and combine thoroughly. Remove from heat and let cool completely.

In small bowl combine broth mix and remaining 1 tablespoon plus 2 teaspoons flour; spread bread crumbs on sheet of wax paper. Form chicken mixture into 8 equal sausage-shaped croquettes; dredge each in seasoned flour, coating all sides, then dip into egg and roll in crumbs, being sure to use all of flour, egg, and crumbs. Arrange croquettes on plate in 1 layer; cover with plastic wrap and refrigerate until chilled (will keep for up to 2 days).

Preheat oven to 375°F. Spray baking sheet with nonstick cooking spray; arrange croquettes on sheet. In small saucepan melt remaining 1 tablespoon plus 2 teaspoons margarine and drizzle an equal amount over each croquette; bake until golden brown, about 15 minutes. Turn croquettes over and bake for 5 minutes longer.

Each serving provides: 3½ Protein Exchanges; 1 Bread Exchange; 2 Fat Exchanges; ¼ Milk Exchange; 5 calories Optional Exchange

Per serving: 378 calories, 33 g protein, 17 g fat, 21 g carbohydrate, 816 mg sodium, 214 mg cholesterol

WEEKLY FOOD DIARY

	MONDAY	TUESDAY	WEDNESDAY	THURSDAY	FRIDAY	SATURDAY	SUNDAY
BREAKFAST FRUIT PROTEIN BREAD FAT MILK OPTIONAL							
LUNCH PROTEIN BREAD VEGETABLES FAT FRUIT MILK OPTIONAL							
DINNER PROTEIN BREAD VEGETABLES FAT FRUIT MILK OPTIONAL							
SNACKS							
DAILY CHECK LIST FRUIT VEG. MILK BREAD FAT PROTEIN OPTIONAL	CALORIES	CALORIES	CALORIES	CALORIES	CALORIES	CALORIES	CALORIES

WEEKLY CHECKLIST OF LIMITED PROTEIN EXCHANGES

EGGS ○○○○

SEMISOFT OR HARD CHEESE ○○○

MEAT GROUP ○○○○○○○○

LIVER ○○○

COMMENTS:

MONDAY
4

TUESDAY
5

WEDNESDAY
6

THURSDAY
7

FRIDAY
8

SATURDAY
9

SUNDAY
10

	S	M	T	W	T	F	S
						1	2
F	3	4	5	6	7	8	9
E	10	11	12	13	14	15	16
B	17	18	19	20	21	22	23
	24	25	26	27	28		

	S	M	T	W	T	F	S
						1	2
M	3	4	5	6	7	8	9
A	10	11	12	13	14	15	16
R	17	18	19	20	21	22	23
	24	25	26	27	28	29	30
	31						

	S	M	T	W	T	F	S
		1	2	3	4	5	6
A	7	8	9	10	11	12	13
P	14	15	16	17	18	19	20
R	21	22	23	24	25	26	27
	28	29	30				

Tuna and Diced Tomato in a Pita Pocket

Vegetable-Cheddar Salad

Reduced-Calorie Chocolate Pudding
with Banana Slices

Coffee with Cinnamon Stick

HELPFUL HINTS: *Vary this week's recipe* by using (1) Swiss cheese instead of Cheddar; (2) 1 cup of blanched cauliflower florets instead of 1 cup of the broccoli; (3) sesame, caraway, or poppy seed instead of sunflower seed.

Vary the menu by (1) adding 2 medium apricots, pitted and sliced, and chopped scallion to the tuna; (2) substituting salmon for tuna; (3) using leftover sliced or diced skinned chicken, turkey or ham instead of tuna.

To speed up preparation, blanch the broccoli ahead of time and refrigerate it.

AWORD FROM JEAN NIDETCH: "Be steadfast" is the password. Perhaps you're faced with insistent hosts pushing you to "forget" your weight-loss plan because it's the weekend (holiday, birthday, anniversary, you name it). If half the time you give in, or murmur a feeble "Welllll . . ."—if even your "No" has question marks fluttering around it, people will get the message that all you need is a little coaxing. On the other hand, if you voice a steadfast "No, thanks" *every single time,* they'll get the message that you mean what you say.

PLAN FOR SUCCESS

What I succeeded at this week _____

_____

Goal for next week _____

Vegetable-Cheddar Salad

Makes 2 servings

2 cups broccoli florets, blanched
1 cup sliced mushrooms
2 ounces sharp Cheddar cheese, shredded
2 teaspoons sunflower seed
1 tablespoon each minced fresh chives,*
    lemon juice, and olive oil
¼ teaspoon each garlic powder and
    powdered mustard
⅛ teaspoon each salt and pepper

In salad bowl combine first 4 ingredients. In small bowl combine remaining ingredients; pour over salad and toss to coat. Cover and refrigerate for 1 hour.

*Freeze-dried chopped chives may be substituted for the minced fresh.

Each serving provides: 1 Protein Exchange; 3 Vegetable Exchanges; 1½ Fat Exchanges; 20 calories Optional Exchange
Per serving: 250 calories, 13 g protein, 18 g fat, 11 g carbohydrate, 357 mg sodium, 30 mg cholesterol

WEEKLY FOOD DIARY

	MONDAY	TUESDAY	WEDNESDAY	THURSDAY	FRIDAY	SATURDAY	SUNDAY
BREAKFAST FRUIT PROTEIN BREAD FAT MILK OPTIONAL							
LUNCH PROTEIN BREAD VEGETABLES FAT FRUIT MILK OPTIONAL							
DINNER PROTEIN BREAD VEGETABLES FAT FRUIT MILK OPTIONAL							
SNACKS							
DAILY CHECK LIST FRUIT VEG. MILK BREAD FAT PROTEIN OPTIONAL	CALORIES	CALORIES	CALORIES	CALORIES	CALORIES	CALORIES	CALORIES

WEEKLY CHECKLIST OF LIMITED PROTEIN EXCHANGES

EGGS ○○○○ ○○○○

SEMISOFT OR HARD CHEESE ○○○○ ○○○○

MEAT GROUP ○○○○○○○○○○○○○

LIVER ○○○○○○

COMMENTS:

MONDAY
11

TUESDAY
12

WEDNESDAY
13

THURSDAY
14

FRIDAY
15

SATURDAY
16

St. Patrick's Day

SUNDAY
17

F E B	S	M	T	W	T	F	S
						1	2
	3	4	5	6	7	8	9
	10	11	12	13	14	15	16
	17	18	19	20	21	22	23
	24	25	26	27	28		

M A R	S	M	T	W	T	F	S
						1	2
	3	4	5	6	7	8	9
	10	11	12	13	14	15	16
	17	18	19	20	21	22	23
	24	25	26	27	28	29	30
	31						

A P R	S	M	T	W	T	F	S
		1	2	3	4	5	6
	7	8	9	10	11	12	13
	14	15	16	17	18	19	20
	21	22	23	24	25	26	27
	28	29	30				

Lentil Stew

Mixed Green Salad with
French Dressing

Canned Peach Half Topped with
Vanilla Dietary Frozen Dessert
and Raspberry Syrup

Coffee or Tea

HELPFUL HINTS: *Avoid adding salt* when cooking lentils or other dried beans; it toughens them and prolongs the cooking time.

How to know when a mixture is at a simmer? Look for slow-rising bubbles and a still surface. And when lifting the cover off a simmering pot, be sure to do it away from you to avoid a steam burn, and do it quickly to prevent condensation from falling back into the pot, diluting the contents.

A WORD FROM JEAN NIDETCH: Spring is on the horizon. Coats are coming off, camouflage time is over. . . . It's the season to reshape your priorities to include a regular regimen of exercise to help those pounds come off faster and trim your body in better proportions. On days when you are pressed for time, divide your routine into two segments. That's better than skipping a day. Walking is one of the least expensive and best all-around forms of exercise. Moreover, it provides a chance to view everything that's starting to bloom (including yourself).

PLAN FOR SUCCESS

What I succeeded at this week _____

_____

Goal for next week _____

Lentil Stew

Makes 4 servings, about 2 cups each

Tasty, filling, and inexpensive, this is a dish whose flavor improves with time. It can be prepared ahead and refrigerated or frozen.

9 ounces rinsed uncooked lentils
1 quart water
12 ounces pared potatoes, diced
1 cup each diced onion, celery,
    and carrot
¼ cup chopped fresh parsley
4 packets instant beef broth and
    seasoning mix
2 garlic cloves, minced
1 bay leaf
⅛ teaspoon ground cumin

In 4-quart saucepan combine lentils and water and bring to a boil. Reduce heat, cover pan, and let simmer until lentils are tender, about 25 minutes.

Add remaining ingredients to lentils and stir to combine; cover and cook over low heat until potatoes are tender, 45 minutes to 1 hour. Remove bay leaf before serving.

Each serving provides: 3 Protein Exchanges; 1 Bread Exchange; 1½ Vegetable Exchanges; 10 calories Optional Exchange
Per serving: 329 calories, 20 g protein, 1 g fat, 63 g carbohydrate, 825 mg sodium, 0 mg cholesterol

WEEKLY FOOD DIARY

	MONDAY	TUESDAY	WEDNESDAY	THURSDAY	FRIDAY	SATURDAY	SUNDAY
BREAKFAST FRUIT PROTEIN BREAD FAT MILK OPTIONAL							
LUNCH PROTEIN BREAD VEGETABLES FAT FRUIT MILK OPTIONAL							
DINNER PROTEIN BREAD VEGETABLES FAT FRUIT MILK OPTIONAL							
SNACKS							

DAILY CHECK LIST

FRUIT
VEG.
MILK
BREAD
FAT
PROTEIN
OPTIONAL

CALORIES (each day)

WEEKLY CHECKLIST OF LIMITED PROTEIN EXCHANGES

EGGS

MEAT GROUP

LIVER

SEMISOFT OR
HARD CHEESE

COMMENTS:

ENGAGEMENTS

MARCH

1985

MONDAY
18

TUESDAY
19

WEDNESDAY
20

THURSDAY
21

FRIDAY
22

SATURDAY
23

SUNDAY
24

	S	M	T	W	T	F	S
F						1	2
E	3	4	5	6	7	8	9
B	10	11	12	13	14	15	16
	17	18	19	20	21	22	23
	24	25	26	27	28		

	S	M	T	W	T	F	S
M						1	2
A	3	4	5	6	7	8	9
R	10	11	12	13	14	15	16
	17	18	19	20	21	22	23
	24	25	26	27	28	29	30
	31						

	S	M	T	W	T	F	S
A		1	2	3	4	5	6
P	7	8	9	10	11	12	13
R	14	15	16	17	18	19	20
	21	22	23	24	25	26	27
	28	29	30				

Baked Chicken Legs

Baked Potato Topped with
Plain Low-Fat Yogurt, Chopped Chives, and
Grated Parmesan Cheese

Steamed Asparagus Spears

Caramel Pears with Cream

Coffee or Tea

HELPFUL HINTS: *As a variation on this week's recipe,* use 1 cup of canned peach slices instead of the pears.

Extend the use of the yogurt topping to other fresh or frozen fruit desserts. Covered, it will keep in the refrigerator for up to 2 days.

A cooking tip: When grating orange peel, be careful not to grate the white pith, which has a bitter taste. The remaining orange can be sectioned or sliced to make a salad with lettuce and onion rings in a vinaigrette dressing.

A WORD FROM JEAN NIDETCH: Spring-cleaning? What an opportune time to rearrange your kitchen so that only the most helpful foods are up front within easy sight and reach. If you must have foods you shouldn't eat on hand, store them where you can't get at them easily. Lower the visibility of see-through boxes and mouth-watering illustrations by storing them backward, so you don't see them. "Out of sight" may not be completely "out of mind," but it sure can help.

PLAN FOR SUCCESS

What I succeeded at this week _____

_____

Goal for next week _____

WEIGHT

RECIPE

WATCHERS

Caramel Pears with Cream

Makes 2 servings

With Easter on the horizon, keep this recipe in mind for a delightful holiday dessert. Select pears that are ripe but not mushy.

2 tablespoons each plain low-fat yogurt
 and thawed frozen dairy whipped topping
½ teaspoon each grated orange peel
 and brandy extract
2 small pears, poached
2 teaspoons each granulated sugar and
 margarine
½ teaspoon vanilla extract
1 tablespoon water

In small bowl combine yogurt, topping, orange peel, and brandy extract; cover and refrigerate until chilled.

Peel, core, and quarter each pear. In small nonstick skillet heat sugar over very low heat until melted and golden, being careful not to let it burn; stir in margarine and vanilla. Add pears and cook, gently stirring constantly and turning each quarter until coated on all sides. Using slotted spoon, transfer 4 quarters to each of 2 dessert dishes; keep warm. Add water to pan juices and, stirring constantly, bring to a boil; pour half of mixture over each portion of pears, then top each with half of yogurt mixture. Serve immediately.

Each serving provides: 1 Fat Exchange; 1 Fruit Exchange; 45 calories Optional Exchange
Per serving: 171 calories, 1 g protein, 6 g fat, 30 g carbohydrate, 54 mg sodium, 1 mg cholesterol

WEEKLY FOOD DIARY

	MONDAY	TUESDAY	WEDNESDAY	THURSDAY	FRIDAY	SATURDAY	SUNDAY
BREAKFAST FRUIT PROTEIN BREAD FAT MILK OPTIONAL							
LUNCH PROTEIN BREAD VEGETABLES FAT FRUIT MILK OPTIONAL							
DINNER PROTEIN BREAD VEGETABLES FAT FRUIT MILK OPTIONAL							
SNACKS							
DAILY CHECK LIST FRUIT VEG. MILK BREAD FAT PROTEIN OPTIONAL	CALORIES	CALORIES	CALORIES	CALORIES	CALORIES	CALORIES	CALORIES

WEEKLY CHECKLIST OF LIMITED PROTEIN EXCHANGES

EGGS ○○○○ ○○○○

MEAT GROUP ○○○○○○ ○○○○○○ ○○○○○

SEMISOFT OR HARD CHEESE ○○○○ ○○○○

LIVER ○○○○

COMMENTS:

MARCH

1 9 8 5

MONDAY
25

TUESDAY
26

WEDNESDAY
27

THURSDAY
28

FRIDAY
29

SATURDAY
30

Palm Sunday

SUNDAY
31

	S	M	T	W	T	F	S
F						1	2
E	3	4	5	6	7	8	9
B	10	11	12	13	14	15	16
	17	18	19	20	21	22	23
	24	25	26	27	28		

	S	M	T	W	T	F	S
M						1	2
A	3	4	5	6	7	8	9
R	10	11	12	13	14	15	16
	17	18	19	20	21	22	23
	24	25	26	27	28	29	30
	31						

	S	M	T	W	T	F	S
A		1	2	3	4	5	6
P	7	8	9	10	11	12	13
R	14	15	16	17	18	19	20
	21	22	23	24	25	26	27
	28	29	30				

WEIGHT MENU WATCHERS

Boneless Leg of Lamb Rosemary

Oven-Roasted Potatoes

Minted Carrots

Melon Wedge with Lemon Slice

Rosé or Red Wine

HELPFUL HINTS: *For a good salad,* combine leftover lamb with white beans, parsley, and scallions in a vinaigrette dressing.

For school or office lunch, freeze sandwiches of leftover lamb and horseradish on rye bread in individual plastic bags. Taken out in the morning, they will thaw in time for lunch.

Cooking tip: A dark roasting pan rather than a light, shiny one is best to cook large cuts of meat or poultry because it absorbs heat, thereby reducing cooking time and facilitating browning.

A WORD FROM JEAN NIDETCH: "April is the cruelest month," so the poet said— and that's especially true for the weight-wary this month, since both Easter and Passover fall in April. One way to steer a straight course on these feast days is to use our slimming versions of traditional recipes; another, if you're a guest, is to bring a gift *you* can enjoy—a basket of fruit, for example, instead of tempting cookies.

PLAN FOR SUCCESS

What I succeeded at this week _____

_____

Goal for next week _____

Boneless Leg of Lamb Rosemary

Makes about 8 servings

Although leg of lamb may seem expensive initially, leftovers can form the base for many other meals or may be frozen in handy individual portions for future use.

1 garlic clove, chopped
½ teaspoon rosemary leaves, crushed
½ teaspoon salt
⅛ teaspoon pepper
3-pound rolled and tied boned leg of lamb

Preheat oven to 450°F. Mash garlic with rosemary, salt, and pepper to form a paste. Using the point of a small knife, cut slits in lamb and fill slits with garlic mixture.

Transfer lamb to rack in roasting pan and insert meat thermometer in center of roast; roast for 15 minutes.

Reduce oven temperature to 325°F. and roast meat until thermometer registers 140°F. for rare, about 1 hour longer; 160°F. for medium, about 1¼ hours longer; or 170°F. for well done, about 1½ hours longer.

To make carving easier, let meat stand for about 10 minutes so juices can set before slicing. Serve 4 ounces sliced lamb per portion.

Each serving provides: 4 Protein Exchanges
Per serving: 219 calories, 32 g protein, 9 g fat, 0.2 g carbohydrate, 214 mg sodium, 113 mg cholesterol

WEEKLY FOOD DIARY

	MONDAY	TUESDAY	WEDNESDAY	THURSDAY	FRIDAY	SATURDAY	SUNDAY
BREAKFAST FRUIT PROTEIN BREAD FAT MILK OPTIONAL							
LUNCH PROTEIN BREAD VEGETABLES FAT FRUIT MILK OPTIONAL							
DINNER PROTEIN BREAD VEGETABLES FAT FRUIT MILK OPTIONAL							
SNACKS							
DAILY CHECK LIST FRUIT VEG. MILK BREAD FAT PROTEIN OPTIONAL	○○○○ ○○○ ○○○ ○○○○ ○○○○○○○ ☐ CALORIES	○○○○ ○○○ ○○○ ○○○○ ○○○○○○○ ☐ CALORIES	○○○○ ○○○ ○○○ ○○○○ ○○○○○○○ ☐ CALORIES	○○○○ ○○○ ○○○ ○○○○ ○○○○○○○ ☐ CALORIES	○○○○ ○○○ ○○○ ○○○○ ○○○○○○○ ☐ CALORIES	○○○○ ○○○ ○○○ ○○○○ ○○○○○○○ ☐ CALORIES	○○○○ ○○○ ○○○ ○○○○ ○○○○○○○ ☐ CALORIES

WEEKLY CHECKLIST OF LIMITED PROTEIN EXCHANGES

EGGS ○○○○
SEMISOFT OR HARD CHEESE ○○○○

MEAT GROUP ○○○○○○○○○○○
LIVER ○○○○○

COMMENTS:

APRIL

1 9 8 5

MONDAY
1

TUESDAY
2

WEDNESDAY
3

THURSDAY
4

Good Friday

FRIDAY
5

Passover begins

SATURDAY
6

Easter Sunday

SUNDAY
7

	S	M	T	W	T	F	S
						1	2
M	3	4	5	6	7	8	9
A	10	11	12	13	14	15	16
R	17	18	19	20	21	22	23
	24	25	26	27	28	29	30
	31						

	S	M	T	W	T	F	S
		1	2	3	4	5	6
A	7	8	9	10	11	12	13
P	14	15	16	17	18	19	20
R	21	22	23	24	25	26	27
	28	29	30				

	S	M	T	W	T	F	S
				1	2	3	4
M	5	6	7	8	9	10	11
A	12	13	14	15	16	17	18
Y	19	20	21	22	23	24	25
	26	27	28	29	30	31	

Chicken or Vegetable Bouillon

Chef's Salad with Tuna and
Reduced-Calorie Russian Dressing
or
Gefilte Fish on Lettuce with Tomato and
Cucumber Slices

Apple Kugel Miniatures

Coffee or Tea

HELPFUL HINTS: *Vary this week's recipe* by using 4 large diced prunes for the raisins and substituting whole wheat or egg matzo for plain matzo.

A versatile treat, Apple Kugel Miniatures, hot from the oven, can be a good accompaniment to a roast chicken, or a delicious dessert, topped with preserves or honey.

A WORD FROM JEAN NIDETCH: Supermarkets may look innocent, but they're laden with snares. (Notice how cookie boxes always seem to be at eye level?) Your best weapon is a shopping list. Keep a grip on it and don't allow yourself to buy anything that isn't written on it. If you base your list on a weekly menu plan, you can cut down on extra expeditions to the store—and avoid further temptations. It's best to avoid shopping when you're hungry; those lures are easier to resist *after* you've eaten. Try to shop with a supportive friend or relative. You're likely to emerge not only successful shoppers but slimmer ones as well.

PLAN FOR SUCCESS

What I succeeded at this week _____

_____

Goal for next week _____

Apple Kugel Miniatures

Makes 4 servings

2 matzo boards, broken into small pieces
½ cup water
1 tablespoon plus 2 teaspoons margarine, divided
1 tablespoon plus 1 teaspoon granulated sugar
2 eggs, separated
2 small apples, cored, pared, and coarsely grated
¼ cup raisins, chopped
¼ teaspoon ground cinnamon
Dash salt

In small bowl combine matzo pieces and water and set aside.

Preheat oven to 350°F. In medium mixing bowl combine 1 tablespoon plus 1 teaspoon margarine with the sugar and, using electric mixer, beat until thoroughly combined; add egg yolks and continue beating until mixture is fluffy. Add fruit, cinnamon, and soaked matzo and beat until well combined.

In separate bowl, using clean beaters, beat egg whites with salt until stiff peaks form; gently fold whites into fruit mixture.

Grease four 6-ounce custard cups with ¼ teaspoon margarine each; spoon ¼ of batter into each cup and bake for 30 to 35 minutes (until lightly browned). Let cool for 10 minutes, then loosen with a spatula and remove from custard cups to a rack to cool. Serve warm or at room temperature.

Each serving provides: ½ Protein Exchange; 1 Bread Exchange; 1 Fat Exchange; 1 Fruit Exchange; 30 calories Optional Exchange

Per serving: 223 calories, 6 g protein, 8 g fat, 33 g carbohydrate, 124 mg sodium, 137 mg cholesterol

WEEKLY FOOD DIARY

	MONDAY	TUESDAY	WEDNESDAY	THURSDAY	FRIDAY	SATURDAY	SUNDAY
BREAKFAST FRUIT PROTEIN BREAD FAT MILK OPTIONAL							
LUNCH PROTEIN BREAD VEGETABLES FAT FRUIT MILK OPTIONAL							
DINNER PROTEIN BREAD VEGETABLES FAT FRUIT MILK OPTIONAL							
SNACKS							
DAILY CHECK LIST FRUIT VEG. MILK BREAD FAT PROTEIN OPTIONAL	CALORIES	CALORIES	CALORIES	CALORIES	CALORIES	CALORIES	CALORIES

WEEKLY CHECKLIST OF LIMITED PROTEIN EXCHANGES

EGGS ○○○○

SEMISOFT OR HARD CHEESE ○○○○

MEAT GROUP ○○○○○○○○○○

LIVER ○○○○○○

COMMENTS:

ENGAGEMENTS

APRIL

1 9 8 5

Easter Monday (Canada)

MONDAY
8

TUESDAY
9

WEDNESDAY
10

THURSDAY
11

FRIDAY
12

SATURDAY
13

SUNDAY
14

	S	M	T	W	T	F	S
						1	2
M	3	4	5	6	7	8	9
A	10	11	12	13	14	15	16
R	17	18	19	20	21	22	23
	24	25	26	27	28	29	30
	31						

	S	M	T	W	T	F	S
		1	2	3	4	5	6
A	7	8	9	10	11	12	13
P	14	15	16	17	18	19	20
R	21	22	23	24	25	26	27
	28	29	30				

	S	M	T	W	T	F	S
				1	2	3	4
M	5	6	7	8	9	10	11
A	12	13	14	15	16	17	18
Y	19	20	21	22	23	24	25
	26	27	28	29	30	31	

WEIGHT

MENU

WATCHERS

Broiled Halibut with Lemon Twist
and Chopped Parsley

Breadsticks

Zucchini Strips Provençale

Mixed Green Salad with Oil and
Vinegar Dressing

Canned Pineapple Slices

Coffee or Tea

HELPFUL HINTS: *For a main dish,* top a serving of Zucchini Strips Provençale with 2 ounces of shredded Swiss or mozzarella cheese and heat under the broiler until the cheese melts. Serve with a green salad and Italian bread.

Instead of the zucchini, use 1 large (1½-pound) eggplant, cut into cubes.

Cooking tip: Oil is at the proper temperature for sautéing when a drop of water added to the skillet sizzles.

A WORD FROM JEAN NIDETCH: Having trouble staying on your diet? Just remember, the best way to climb over a hurdle is step by step. Instead of worrying about how you are going to make it all the way to goal, focus on "making it" today—*each* day. Draw up schedules, and plan how you will cope with each hour: perhaps allow time for chores to give you a feeling of accomplishment, followed by some time off for fun. Dividing any problem into small portions makes it easier to deal with.

PLAN FOR SUCCESS

What I succeeded at this week _____

_____

Goal for next week _____

Zucchini Strips Provençale

Makes 2 servings

1 teaspoon olive oil
½ garlic clove, thinly sliced
¼ cup diced onion
2 medium zucchini (about 5 ounces
    each), cut lengthwise into eighths
1 medium tomato, diced
¼ teaspoon oregano leaves
⅛ teaspoon salt
Dash pepper
1 tablespoon chopped fresh parsley
1½ teaspoons lemon juice
Garnish: parsley sprigs

In 9-inch nonstick skillet heat oil; add garlic and sauté until golden. Remove and discard garlic.

Add onion to same skillet and sauté until translucent. Add remaining vegetables, oregano, salt, and pepper; cover and let simmer until zucchini is tender-crisp, about 5 minutes. Sprinkle mixture with chopped parsley and lemon juice and toss gently to combine; serve garnished with parsley sprigs.

Each serving provides: 3¼ Vegetable Exchanges; ½ Fat Exchange
Per serving: 71 calories, 3 g protein, 3 g fat, 11 g carbohydrate, 147 mg sodium, 0 mg cholesterol

WEEKLY FOOD DIARY

	MONDAY	TUESDAY	WEDNESDAY	THURSDAY	FRIDAY	SATURDAY	SUNDAY
BREAKFAST FRUIT PROTEIN BREAD FAT MILK OPTIONAL							
LUNCH PROTEIN BREAD VEGETABLES FAT FRUIT MILK OPTIONAL							
DINNER PROTEIN BREAD VEGETABLES FAT FRUIT MILK OPTIONAL							
SNACKS							
DAILY CHECK LIST FRUIT VEG. MILK BREAD FAT PROTEIN OPTIONAL CALORIES	○○○○○ ○○○○ ○○○○ ○○○○○○ ○○○○○○○ ○○○○ ▢ CALORIES	○○○○○ ○○○○ ○○○○ ○○○○○○ ○○○○○○○ ○○○○ ▢ CALORIES	○○○○○ ○○○○ ○○○○ ○○○○○○ ○○○○○○○ ○○○○ ▢ CALORIES	○○○○○ ○○○○ ○○○○ ○○○○○○ ○○○○○○○ ○○○○ ▢ CALORIES	○○○○○ ○○○○ ○○○○ ○○○○○○ ○○○○○○○ ○○○○ ▢ CALORIES	○○○○○ ○○○○ ○○○○ ○○○○○○ ○○○○○○○ ○○○○ ▢ CALORIES	○○○○○ ○○○○ ○○○○ ○○○○○○ ○○○○○○○ ○○○○ ▢ CALORIES

WEEKLY CHECKLIST OF LIMITED PROTEIN EXCHANGES

EGGS ○○○○

SEMISOFT OR HARD CHEESE ○○○

MEAT GROUP ○○○○○○○○○

LIVER ○○○○○○

COMMENTS:

MONDAY
15

TUESDAY
16

WEDNESDAY
17

THURSDAY
18

FRIDAY
19

SATURDAY
20

SUNDAY
21

	S	M	T	W	T	F	S
						1	2
M	3	4	5	6	7	8	9
A	10	11	12	13	14	15	16
R	17	18	19	20	21	22	23
	24	25	26	27	28	29	30
	31						

	S	M	T	W	T	F	S
		1	2	3	4	5	6
A	7	8	9	10	11	12	13
P	14	15	16	17	18	19	20
R	21	22	23	24	25	26	27
	28	29	30				

	S	M	T	W	T	F	S
				1	2	3	4
M	5	6	7	8	9	10	11
A	12	13	14	15	16	17	18
Y	19	20	21	22	23	24	25
	26	27	28	29	30	31	

WEIGHT

MENU

WATCHERS

Sautéed Chicken Livers with
Sliced Onions and Mushroom Caps

Vegetable Risotto Parmesan

Steamed Broccoli Spears

Vanilla Dietary Frozen Dessert
with Mandarin Orange Sections

Red, White, or Rosé Wine

HELPFUL HINTS: *Transform Vegetable Risotto Parmesan to a main dish* by adding to each serving 3 ounces of diced cooked seafood, skinned chicken, or ham.

For a side dish, use Vegetable Risotto Parmesan as a stuffing for steamed green peppers or large cooked mushroom caps.

Vary the recipe by substituting ½ cup diced zucchini, mushrooms, red bell pepper, or broccoli spears for the carrot and green pepper.

A WORD FROM JEAN NIDETCH: "When I'm slim I'll _____ " (fill in the dream of your choice). But why wait? Getting a taste of what you want can inspire you to keep going, and keep you from other tastes! So if you dream of a super social life, but meanwhile you're a shy stay-at-homer, *now* is the time to join a group where you can meet new people. The advantage to this "dress rehearsal" is that when you get to goal, you'll feel more at home there . . . and be more likely to make it permanent.

PLAN FOR SUCCESS

What I succeeded at this week _____

_____

Goal for next week _____

Vegetable Risotto Parmesan

Makes 2 servings

2 teaspoons peanut oil
¼ cup each diced onion and celery
2 tablespoons each diced carrot and
    green bell pepper
½ teaspoon minced fresh garlic
1 cup water
1 ounce uncooked regular long-grain rice
1 packet instant chicken broth and
    seasoning mix
1½ teaspoons grated Parmesan cheese

In small saucepan heat oil; add vegetables and garlic and cook, stirring constantly, until vegetables are tender-crisp. Stir in water, rice, and broth mix; stirring constantly, bring to a boil. Reduce heat, cover pan, and let simmer, stirring occasionally, until all moisture is absorbed, about 20 minutes; serve sprinkled with Parmesan cheese.

Each serving provides: ½ Bread Exchange; ¾ Vegetable Exchange; 1 Fat Exchange; 15 calories Optional Exchange

Per serving: 119 calories, 3 g protein, 5 g fat, 16 g carbohydrate, 466 mg sodium, 1 mg cholesterol

WEEKLY FOOD DIARY

	MONDAY	TUESDAY	WEDNESDAY	THURSDAY	FRIDAY	SATURDAY	SUNDAY
BREAKFAST FRUIT PROTEIN BREAD FAT MILK OPTIONAL							
LUNCH PROTEIN BREAD VEGETABLES FAT FRUIT MILK OPTIONAL							
DINNER PROTEIN BREAD VEGETABLES FAT FRUIT MILK OPTIONAL							
SNACKS							
DAILY CHECK LIST FRUIT VEG. MILK BREAD FAT PROTEIN OPTIONAL	○○○○○ ○○○○○ ○○○○ ○○○○○ ○○○○○ ○○○○○ ☐ CALORIES	○○○○○ ○○○○○ ○○○○ ○○○○○ ○○○○○ ○○○○○ ☐ CALORIES	○○○ ○○○ ○○○ ○○○ ○○○○ ○○○○○ ☐ CALORIES	○○○ ○○○ ○○○ ○○○ ○○○○ ○○○○○ ☐ CALORIES	○○○ ○○○ ○○○ ○○○ ○○○○ ○○○○○ ☐ CALORIES	○○○ ○○○ ○○○ ○○○ ○○○○ ○○○○○ ☐ CALORIES	○○○ ○○○ ○○○ ○○○ ○○○○ ○○○○○ ☐ CALORIES

WEEKLY CHECKLIST OF LIMITED PROTEIN EXCHANGES

EGGS ○○○○

SEMISOFT OR HARD CHEESE ○○○○

MEAT GROUP ○○○○○○○○○○○○○

LIVER ○○○○

COMMENTS:

APRIL

1 9 8 5

MONDAY
22

TUESDAY
23

WEDNESDAY
24

THURSDAY
25

FRIDAY
26

SATURDAY
27

SUNDAY
28

	S	M	T	W	T	F	S
MAR						1	2
	3	4	5	6	7	8	9
	10	11	12	13	14	15	16
	17	18	19	20	21	22	23
	24	25	26	27	28	29	30
	31						

	S	M	T	W	T	F	S
APR		1	2	3	4	5	6
	7	8	9	10	11	12	13
	14	15	16	17	18	19	20
	21	22	23	24	25	26	27
	28	29	30				

	S	M	T	W	T	F	S
MAY				1	2	3	4
	5	6	7	8	9	10	11
	12	13	14	15	16	17	18
	19	20	21	22	23	24	25
	26	27	28	29	30	31	

WEIGHT

MENU

WATCHERS

Stuffed Veal Rolls

Steamed Red and Green Bell Pepper Strips

Belgian Endive Salad with
Fresh Lemon Juice and Herbs

Strawberries with
Instant Whipped Cream

Coffee or Tea

HELPFUL HINTS: *In buying veal,* look for pale pink cuts; the redder the veal, the older and tougher it is. To cut the cost of preparing this recipe, purchase cutlets on sale and freeze them.

To pound cutlets, place between two sheets of plastic wrap and use the flat side of a meat mallet or the bottom of a saucepan.

Time-saving tip: Potato stuffing can be prepared in advance and refrigerated. Cutlets can be stuffed in the morning and refrigerated until ready to be sautéed.

A WORD FROM JEAN NIDETCH: "I've already gone off my diet, so I might as well forget about the rest of today." Familiar words? They're also very costly ones. They give permission for a momentary lapse to become a day-long (week-long?) binge. Losing out on the rest of a day not only costs pounds, it undermines your discipline. Better to assert yourself and decide: "My next choice will be better." That's the way to create a *lifelong* pattern of success.

PLAN FOR SUCCESS

What I succeeded at this week _____

_____

Goal for next week _____

Stuffed Veal Rolls

Makes 2 servings

Although veal cutlets may seem expensive, they have almost no waste in terms of bone or fat.

1 tablespoon plus 1 teaspoon margarine, divided
1 cup thinly sliced onions
1 teaspoon minced fresh garlic
1 cup thinly sliced mushrooms
Dash each salt and pepper
3 ounces peeled cooked potato, diced
2 tablespoons chopped fresh parsley, divided
2 teaspoons grated Parmesan or Romano cheese
2 veal cutlets (5 ounces each), pounded
    to ¼-inch thickness
½ cup dry white wine
¼ cup prepared instant chicken broth (prepared
    according to packet directions)

In 9-inch nonstick skillet heat 2 teaspoons margarine over medium heat until bubbly and hot; add onions and garlic and sauté for 2 minutes (*be careful not to burn*). Add mushrooms, salt, and pepper and continue cooking until most of liquid has evaporated, about 5 minutes.

Transfer vegetable mixture to bowl; add diced potato, 1 tablespoon parsley, and the cheese and stir to combine. Mound half of potato mixture onto each cutlet and roll cutlet to enclose filling, folding in edges; secure each roll with a round toothpick.

In same skillet heat remaining 2 teaspoons margarine over medium heat until bubbly and hot; add veal rolls and cook, turning occasionally, until browned on all sides. Remove veal to a warm serving platter, reserving any pan juices; remove and discard toothpicks and keep veal warm.

Add wine and broth to same skillet; cook over high heat, stirring occasionally and scraping particles from sides and bottom of pan, until sauce is slightly thickened. Pour over veal rolls, sprinkle with remaining tablespoon parsley, and serve immediately.

Each serving provides: 4 Protein Exchanges; ½ Bread Exchange; 2 Vegetable Exchanges; 2 Fat Exchanges; 70 calories Optional Exchange

Per serving: 445 calories, 35 g protein, 21 g fat, 19 g carbohydrate, 417 mg sodium, 116 mg cholesterol

WEEKLY FOOD DIARY

	MONDAY	TUESDAY	WEDNESDAY	THURSDAY	FRIDAY	SATURDAY	SUNDAY
BREAKFAST FRUIT PROTEIN BREAD FAT MILK OPTIONAL							
LUNCH PROTEIN BREAD VEGETABLES FAT FRUIT MILK OPTIONAL							
DINNER PROTEIN BREAD VEGETABLES FAT FRUIT MILK OPTIONAL							
SNACKS							
DAILY CHECK LIST FRUIT VEG. MILK BREAD FAT PROTEIN OPTIONAL	○○○ ○○○ ○○○ ○○○○○○○ CALORIES	○○○ ○○○ ○○○ ○○○○○○○ CALORIES	○○○ ○○○ ○○○ ○○○○○○○ CALORIES	○○○ ○○○ ○○○ ○○○○○○○ CALORIES	○○○ ○○○ ○○○ ○○○○○○○ CALORIES	○○○ ○○○ ○○○ ○○○○○○○ CALORIES	○○○ ○○○ ○○○ ○○○○○○○ CALORIES

WEEKLY CHECKLIST OF LIMITED PROTEIN EXCHANGES

EGGS ○○○○

SEMISOFT OR ○○○○
HARD CHEESE

MEAT GROUP ○○○○○○○○○○○

LIVER ○○○○○○

COMMENTS:

APRIL
MAY

1 9 8 5

MONDAY
29

TUESDAY
30

WEDNESDAY
1

THURSDAY
2

FRIDAY
3

SATURDAY
4

SUNDAY
5

	S	M	T	W	T	F	S
M						1	2
A	3	4	5	6	7	8	9
	10	11	12	13	14	15	16
R	17	18	19	20	21	22	23
	24	25	26	27	28	29	30
	31						

	S	M	T	W	T	F	S
		1	2	3	4	5	6
A	7	8	9	10	11	12	13
P	14	15	16	17	18	19	20
R	21	22	23	24	25	26	27
	28	29	30				

	S	M	T	W	T	F	S
				1	2	3	4
M	5	6	7	8	9	10	11
A	12	13	14	15	16	17	18
Y	19	20	21	22	23	24	25
	26	27	28	29	30	31	

Mimosa

Poached Eggs Florentine

Broiled Canadian-Style Bacon

Tomato Wedges on Boston Lettuce Leaves

Cinnamon Coffee Topped with
Instant Whipped Cream

HELPFUL HINTS: *To vary the recipe,* use Cheddar cheese instead of Swiss; add 1 ounce of sliced Canadian-style bacon or cooked ham to each muffin half; poach eggs in water flavored with tarragon vinegar.

Cooking tips: For successful poached eggs, use only fresh high-quality eggs. Break each egg into a cup before slipping it into simmering, *not bubbling,* water. *To reheat,* place in lightly salted warm water and heat slowly. Remove gently with a slotted spoon.

A WORD FROM JEAN NIDETCH: What could be more appropriate for a mother on a slenderizing program than a gift that says, "I not only appreciate *you,* but also what you're trying to accomplish." That gift might be a dinner out in a restaurant that offers the right kind of food, or it could be a special low-calorie breakfast in bed, with a rose to brighten the tray. Or how about a certificate that promises to take over the food-related kitchen chores for a week? That kind of supportiveness could make it seem like Mother's Year.

PLAN FOR SUCCESS

What I succeeded at this week _____

_____

Goal for next week _____

Poached Eggs Florentine

Makes 2 servings

This spinach mixture can also double as an omelet filling.

2 teaspoons margarine
1 tablespoon minced onion
1 garlic clove, minced
½ cup well-drained cooked chopped spinach
2 teaspoons all-purpose flour
½ cup skim milk
2 ounces Swiss cheese, shredded
⅛ teaspoon salt
Dash ground nutmeg
1 English muffin, split and toasted
2 eggs, poached (hot)

In small skillet heat margarine over medium-high heat until bubbly and hot; add onion and garlic and sauté, stirring constantly, until onion is translucent. Add spinach and stir to combine; sprinkle flour over mixture, stirring to combine. Gradually stir in milk and bring to a boil. Reduce heat to medium and cook, stirring constantly, until combined and mixture thickens. Reduce heat to low and add cheese, salt, and nutmeg; cook, stirring, until cheese is melted. Spoon half of mixture over each muffin half and top each with 1 poached egg; serve immediately.

Each serving provides: 2 Protein Exchanges; 1 Bread Exchange; ½ Vegetable Exchange; 1 Fat Exchange; ¼ Milk Exchange; 10 calories Optional Exchange

Per serving: 330 calories, 20 g protein, 18 g fat, 22 g carbohydrate, 605 mg sodium, 300 mg cholesterol

WEEKLY FOOD DIARY

	MONDAY	TUESDAY	WEDNESDAY	THURSDAY	FRIDAY	SATURDAY	SUNDAY
BREAKFAST FRUIT PROTEIN BREAD FAT MILK OPTIONAL							
LUNCH PROTEIN BREAD VEGETABLES FAT FRUIT MILK OPTIONAL							
DINNER PROTEIN BREAD VEGETABLES FAT FRUIT MILK OPTIONAL							
SNACKS							

DAILY CHECK LIST

FRUIT
VEG.
MILK
BREAD
FAT
PROTEIN
OPTIONAL

CALORIES (Monday) CALORIES (Tuesday) CALORIES (Wednesday) CALORIES (Thursday) CALORIES (Friday) CALORIES (Saturday) CALORIES (Sunday)

WEEKLY CHECKLIST OF LIMITED PROTEIN EXCHANGES

EGGS

SEMISOFT OR HARD CHEESE

MEAT GROUP

LIVER

COMMENTS:

MAY

MONDAY
6

TUESDAY
7

WEDNESDAY
8

THURSDAY
9

FRIDAY
10

SATURDAY
11

Mother's Day

SUNDAY
12

	S	M	T	W	T	F	S
A P R		1	2	3	4	5	6
	7	8	9	10	11	12	13
	14	15	16	17	18	19	20
	21	22	23	24	25	26	27
	28	29	30				

	S	M	T	W	T	F	S
M A Y				1	2	3	4
	5	6	7	8	9	10	11
	12	13	14	15	16	17	18
	19	20	21	22	23	24	25
	26	27	28	29	30	31	

	S	M	T	W	T	F	S
J U N E							1
	2	3	4	5	6	7	8
	9	10	11	12	13	14	15
	16	17	18	19	20	21	22
	23	24	25	26	27	28	29
	30						

Broiled Pork Chop

Long-Grain Rice with Toasted
Sesame Seed

Oriental Stir-Fry

Cantaloupe with Lemon Wedge

Coffee or Tea

HELPFUL HINTS: *For a main dish,* add 12 ounces of sliced or diced tofu and 12 ounces of cooked seafood or skinned and boned cooked poultry to the Oriental Stir-Fry recipe while vegetables are steaming.

To vary the recipe, for 1 cup of any vegetable substitute 1 cup of broccoli florets, pea pods, shredded cabbage, sliced zucchini, or sliced mushrooms.

When stir-frying, cut ingredients in similar-size pieces to ensure even cooking and tender-crisp texture. Add tenderer vegetables last.

Leftover tip: Add leftover Oriental Stir-Fry to chicken or beef broth for an instant vegetable soup.

A WORD FROM JEAN NIDETCH: Dining alone? Don't succumb to a haphazard sorry-for-yourself meal. Instead, make it an occasion. Use decorative linens, a cloth napkin, and your finest china, silver, and glassware. Put a flower in a bud vase, and dine by candlelight to music. Feed the feeling that you are special because it leads to valuing yourself more . . . the first step to success.

PLAN FOR SUCCESS

What I succeeded at this week _____

_____

Goal for next week _____

Oriental Stir-Fry

Makes 4 servings

1 tablespoon plus 1 teaspoon peanut oil
3 cups diagonally sliced asparagus (woody ends trimmed)*
1 cup each diagonally sliced carrots and celery
1 cup thinly sliced onions
1 medium red bell pepper, cut into thin strips
1 garlic clove, minced
¾ cup hot water
2 teaspoons each dry sherry and oyster sauce
1 packet instant beef broth and seasoning mix
1 teaspoon cornstarch

Heat large wok or 12-inch skillet; add oil and tilt wok (or skillet) to coat evenly with oil. Add vegetables, one at a time in order listed, stir-frying each for 1 minute; add garlic and stir-fry for about 1 minute longer. In measuring cup or bowl combine remaining ingredients, stirring to dissolve cornstarch; pour over vegetables, stirring to combine. Cover wok (or skillet) and let steam until vegetables are tender-crisp or done to taste.

*About 1 pound of medium asparagus stalks will yield 3 cups sliced.

Each serving provides: 3½ Vegetable Exchanges; 1 Fat Exchange; 15 calories Optional Exchange
Per serving: 120 calories, 5 g protein, 5 g fat, 16 g carbohydrate, 367 mg sodium, 0 mg cholesterol

WEEKLY FOOD DIARY

	MONDAY	TUESDAY	WEDNESDAY	THURSDAY	FRIDAY	SATURDAY	SUNDAY
BREAKFAST FRUIT PROTEIN BREAD FAT MILK OPTIONAL							
LUNCH PROTEIN BREAD VEGETABLES FAT FRUIT MILK OPTIONAL							
DINNER PROTEIN BREAD VEGETABLES FAT FRUIT MILK OPTIONAL							
SNACKS							
DAILY CHECK LIST FRUIT VEG. MILK BREAD FAT PROTEIN OPTIONAL	CALORIES	CALORIES	CALORIES	CALORIES	CALORIES	CALORIES	CALORIES

WEEKLY CHECKLIST OF LIMITED PROTEIN EXCHANGES

EGGS ○○○
SEMISOFT OR HARD CHEESE ○○○

MEAT GROUP ○○○○○○○○○
LIVER ○○○

COMMENTS:

MAY

1985

MONDAY
13

TUESDAY
14

Weight Watchers 22nd Anniversary

WEDNESDAY
15

THURSDAY
16

FRIDAY
17

Armed Forces Day

SATURDAY
18

SUNDAY
19

	S	M	T	W	T	F	S
		1	2	3	4	5	6
A	7	8	9	10	11	12	13
P	14	15	16	17	18	19	20
R	21	22	23	24	25	26	27
	28	29	30				

	S	M	T	W	T	F	S
				1	2	3	4
M	5	6	7	8	9	10	11
A	12	13	14	15	16	17	18
Y	19	20	21	22	23	24	25
	26	27	28	29	30	31	

	S	M	T	W	T	F	S
J							1
U	2	3	4	5	6	7	8
N	9	10	11	12	13	14	15
E	16	17	18	19	20	21	22
	23	24	25	26	27	28	29
	30						

Crispy Liver with Sweet 'n' Sour Sauce

Stir-Fried Pea Pods and Mushroom Caps

Bean Sprouts on Lettuce Leaves with
Oil and Wine Vinegar Dressing

Kiwi Fruit

Herb Tea

HELPFUL HINTS: *Vary this week's recipe* by using chicken livers instead of calf's liver. Use Sweet 'n' Sour Sauce with baked or broiled chicken, roast pork, or boiled shrimp.

Economy tip: Stock-pile chicken livers for a budget version of the recipe. When you buy whole chickens, freeze the livers until you have collected enough for a meal.

Cooking tips: Wipe liver with a damp cloth before cooking and remove outer membrane and any veins. During broiling, use tongs to turn liver. Do not overcook; liver should be brown on the outside, pink on the inside.

A WORD FROM JEAN NIDETCH: "One bite won't hurt" is a dangerous message that we sometimes give to ourselves. The question isn't "How much it can hurt," but "Will it *help?*" If you don't believe that "little bites" can sabotage your efforts, just keep a written record of every bite and sip. You'll be amazed to discover that they can add up to as much as an extra meal.

PLAN FOR SUCCESS

What I succeeded at this week _____

_____

Goal for next week _____

Crispy Liver with Sweet 'n' Sour Sauce

Makes 2 servings

⅓ cup plus 2 teaspoons seasoned dried bread crumbs
1 packet instant onion broth and seasoning mix
10 ounces calf's liver, cut into 1 x 2-inch strips
2 tablespoons water
1 tablespoon plus 1 teaspoon reduced-calorie apricot
    spread (16 calories per 2 teaspoons)
1 tablespoon teriyaki sauce
1 teaspoon lemon juice

Spray broiling pan with nonstick cooking spray and set aside. In bowl combine bread crumbs and broth mix; dredge liver in crumb mixture and transfer to sprayed pan. Broil 3 inches from heat source until browned, about 4 minutes; turn liver strips over and broil just until other side is browned (*do not overcook*).

While liver is broiling, in small saucepan combine remaining ingredients and heat; serve as dipping sauce with liver.

Each serving provides: 4 Protein Exchanges; 1 Bread Exchange; 20 calories Optional Exchange
Per serving: 302 calories, 30 g protein, 8 g fat, 26 g carbohydrate, 1,462 mg sodium, 426 mg cholesterol

WEEKLY FOOD DIARY

	MONDAY	TUESDAY	WEDNESDAY	THURSDAY	FRIDAY	SATURDAY	SUNDAY
BREAKFAST FRUIT PROTEIN BREAD FAT MILK OPTIONAL							
LUNCH PROTEIN BREAD VEGETABLES FAT FRUIT MILK OPTIONAL							
DINNER PROTEIN BREAD VEGETABLES FAT FRUIT MILK OPTIONAL							
SNACKS							
DAILY CHECK LIST FRUIT VEG. MILK BREAD FAT PROTEIN OPTIONAL	○○○ ○○○ ○○○ ○○○ ○○○ ○○○○○○○ □ CALORIES	○○○ ○○○ ○○○ ○○○ ○○○ ○○○○○○○ □ CALORIES	○○○ ○○○ ○○○ ○○○ ○○○ ○○○○○○○ □ CALORIES	○○○ ○○○ ○○○ ○○○ ○○○ ○○○○○○○ □ CALORIES	○○○ ○○○ ○○○ ○○○ ○○○ ○○○○○○○ □ CALORIES	○○○ ○○○ ○○○ ○○○ ○○○ ○○○○○○○ □ CALORIES	○○○ ○○○ ○○○ ○○○ ○○○ ○○○○○○○ □ CALORIES

WEEKLY CHECKLIST OF LIMITED PROTEIN EXCHANGES

EGGS ○○○ ○○○ ○○○

SEMISOFT OR HARD CHEESE ○○○ ○○○ ○

MEAT GROUP ○○○○○○○○○○

LIVER ○○○○○

COMMENTS:

MAY

Victoria Day (Canada)

MONDAY
20

TUESDAY
21

WEDNESDAY
22

THURSDAY
23

FRIDAY
24

SATURDAY
25

SUNDAY
26

	S	M	T	W	T	F	S
		1	2	3	4	5	6
A	7	8	9	10	11	12	13
P	14	15	16	17	18	19	20
R	21	22	23	24	25	26	27
	28	29	30				

	S	M	T	W	T	F	S
				1	2	3	4
M	5	6	7	8	9	10	11
A	12	13	14	15	16	17	18
Y	19	20	21	22	23	24	25
	26	27	28	29	30	31	

	S	M	T	W	T	F	S
J							1
U	2	3	4	5	6	7	8
N	9	10	11	12	13	14	15
E	16	17	18	19	20	21	22
	23	24	25	26	27	28	29
	30						

Oven-Barbecued Chicken

Steamed Sliced Carrots

Roquefort-Pasta Salad

Fresh Fruit Compote Topped with
Plain Low-Fat Yogurt and Cinnamon

Iced Tea with Mint Sprig

HELPFUL HINTS: *Vary this week's recipe* by substituting (1) 1 cup cooked broccoli florets for the green beans; (2) 4 ounces skinned and diced cooked turkey or chicken for the hard-cooked eggs; (3) any kind of cooked small pasta for the spinach macaroni.

To save time, cook and chill pasta, green beans, and eggs in advance.

To ripen fresh tomatoes, let stand in brown paper bag at room temperature for 1 or 2 days.

A WORD FROM JEAN NIDETCH: "How can I cook without tasting?" If that's an echo of *your* voice, tune in to other messages. Ask someone else to be the taster. Or follow recipe measurements without taking the instruction "to taste" literally. Worried that a dish may not be salty enough? These days people aware of good nutrition know that sodium intake should be reduced, so let everyone add the amount he or she prefers at the table. And if all else fails, who says tasting has to mean *swallowing?*

PLAN FOR SUCCESS

What I succeeded at this week _____

_____

Goal for next week _____

Roquefort-Pasta Salad

Makes 4 servings

2 cups cooked spinach elbow macaroni,
    chilled
1 cup cooked cut green beans, chilled
1 medium tomato, chopped
1 ounce Roquefort cheese
2 tablespoons mayonnaise
¼ cup plain low-fat yogurt
Dash each garlic powder and pepper
4 eggs, hard-cooked, chilled, and cut
    into quarters

In salad bowl combine macaroni, green beans, and tomato; set aside. In small mixing bowl, using a fork, mash together cheese and mayonnaise until cheese is softened and has a spreadlike consistency; stir in yogurt, garlic powder, and pepper. Pour dressing over macaroni mixture and toss well to combine; serve garnished with egg quarters.

Each serving provides: 1 Protein Exchange; 1 Bread Exchange; 1 Vegetable Exchange; 1½ Fat Exchanges; 30 calories Optional Exchange

Per serving: 263 calories, 12 g protein, 15 g fat, 21 g carbohydrate, 250 mg sodium, 305 mg cholesterol

WEEKLY FOOD DIARY

	MONDAY	TUESDAY	WEDNESDAY	THURSDAY	FRIDAY	SATURDAY	SUNDAY
BREAKFAST FRUIT PROTEIN BREAD FAT MILK OPTIONAL							
LUNCH PROTEIN BREAD VEGETABLES FAT FRUIT MILK OPTIONAL							
DINNER PROTEIN BREAD VEGETABLES FAT FRUIT MILK OPTIONAL							
SNACKS							
DAILY CHECK LIST FRUIT VEG. MILK BREAD FAT PROTEIN OPTIONAL	○○○○○○○ CALORIES	○○○○○○○ CALORIES	○○○○○○○ CALORIES	○○○○○○○ CALORIES	○○○○○○○ CALORIES	○○○○○○○ CALORIES	○○○○○○○ CALORIES

WEEKLY CHECKLIST OF LIMITED PROTEIN EXCHANGES

EGGS ○○○○

SEMISOFT OR HARD CHEESE ○○○

MEAT GROUP ○○○○○○○○○

LIVER ○○○

COMMENTS:

E N G A G E M E N T S

MAY
JUNE

1 9 8 5

Memorial Day (observed)

MONDAY
27

TUESDAY
28

WEDNESDAY
29

Memorial Day

THURSDAY
30

FRIDAY
31

SATURDAY
1

SUNDAY
2

	S	M	T	W	T	F	S
APR		1	2	3	4	5	6
	7	8	9	10	11	12	13
	14	15	16	17	18	19	20
	21	22	23	24	25	26	27
	28	29	30				

	S	M	T	W	T	F	S
MAY				1	2	3	4
	5	6	7	8	9	10	11
	12	13	14	15	16	17	18
	19	20	21	22	23	24	25
	26	27	28	29	30	31	

	S	M	T	W	T	F	S
JUNE							1
	2	3	4	5	6	7	8
	9	10	11	12	13	14	15
	16	17	18	19	20	21	22
	23	24	25	26	27	28	29
	30						

Frankfurters en Croûte

Sauerkraut

Sautéed Onions with Paprika

Tossed Salad with Reduced-Calorie
Creamy Cucumber Dressing

Cherries

Coffee or Tea

HELPFUL HINTS: *For delicious hors d'oeuvres,* slice Frankfurters en Croûte into 1-inch pieces, insert toothpicks, and arrange decoratively on a plate.

For hamburger en croûte, shape 10 ounces of ground beef into 4 equal sausage-shaped rolls and broil. Then proceed as directed in the second paragraph of the recipe.

A WORD FROM JEAN NIDETCH: Want a clue to attaining a goal? *Look for ways to succeed, not ways to fail.* Example: You customarily get your summer exercise by swimming in the local pool, but you discover it's not going to open this season. Do you give up, or do you look for ways to swim around that hurdle? Like checking the phone book for the location of another pool. Or arranging to get to a beach. Or deciding this is an opportunity to learn a new sport, like tennis. What it boils down to is: Are you looking for a way to be part of the *problem*—or part of the *solution?*

PLAN FOR SUCCESS

What I succeeded at this week _____

_____

Goal for next week _____

Frankfurters en Croûte

Makes 4 servings

Chicken or turkey frankfurters as well as beef frankfurters can also be used in this recipe.

    4 ready-to-bake refrigerated buttermilk
        flaky biscuits (1 ounce each)
    4 frankfurters (2 ounces each)
    4 ounces Cheddar cheese, shredded
    2 tablespoons plus 2 teaspoons ketchup
    1 tablespoon plus 1 teaspoon each prepared
        mustard and pickle relish

Preheat oven to 375°F. Roll each biscuit between 2 sheets of wax paper, forming four 6-inch circles; set 1 frankfurter in center of each circle.

In small bowl combine remaining ingredients; spread ¼ of mixture over each frankfurter.

Fold dough over ends of each frankfurter, then roll to enclose, forming 4 encased frankfurters; using wet fingertips, pinch edges of dough to seal.

Spray baking sheet with nonstick cooking spray and place frankfurters, seam-side down, on sheet; bake until thoroughly heated and dough is browned, 10 to 15 minutes.

Each serving provides: 3 Protein Exchanges; 1 Bread Exchange; 20 calories Optional Exchange
Per serving: 397 calories, 16 g protein, 28 g fat, 20 g carbohydrate, 1,278 mg sodium, 58 mg cholesterol

WEEKLY FOOD DIARY

	MONDAY	TUESDAY	WEDNESDAY	THURSDAY	FRIDAY	SATURDAY	SUNDAY
BREAKFAST FRUIT PROTEIN BREAD FAT MILK OPTIONAL							
LUNCH PROTEIN BREAD VEGETABLES FAT FRUIT MILK OPTIONAL							
DINNER PROTEIN BREAD VEGETABLES FAT FRUIT MILK OPTIONAL							
SNACKS							
DAILY CHECK LIST FRUIT VEG. MILK BREAD FAT PROTEIN OPTIONAL	○○ ○○○ ○○○ ○○○ ○○○○○○○ □ CALORIES	○○ ○○○ ○○○ ○○○ ○○○○○○○ □ CALORIES	○○ ○○○ ○○○ ○○○ ○○○○○○○ □ CALORIES	○○ ○○○ ○○○ ○○○ ○○○○○○○ □ CALORIES	○○ ○○○ ○○○ ○○○ ○○○○○○○ □ CALORIES	○○ ○○○ ○○○ ○○○ ○○○○○○○ □ CALORIES	○○ ○○○ ○○○ ○○○ ○○○○○○○ □ CALORIES

WEEKLY CHECKLIST OF LIMITED PROTEIN EXCHANGES

EGGS ○○○ ○○○ MEAT GROUP ○○○○○○○○○○

SEMISOFT OR HARD CHEESE ○○○ ○○ LIVER ○○○

COMMENTS:

JUNE

1985

MONDAY
3

TUESDAY
4

WEDNESDAY
5

THURSDAY
6

FRIDAY
7

SATURDAY
8

SUNDAY
9

	S	M	T	W	T	F	S
MAY				1	2	3	4
	5	6	7	8	9	10	11
	12	13	14	15	16	17	18
	19	20	21	22	23	24	25
	26	27	28	29	30	31	

	S	M	T	W	T	F	S
JUNE							1
	2	3	4	5	6	7	8
	9	10	11	12	13	14	15
	16	17	18	19	20	21	22
	23	24	25	26	27	28	29
	30						

	S	M	T	W	T	F	S
JULY		1	2	3	4	5	6
	7	8	9	10	11	12	13
	14	15	16	17	18	19	20
	21	22	23	24	25	26	27
	28	29	30	31			

Sautéed Scallops Provençale

Parslied Rice

Steamed Zucchini Slices

Honeydew Wedge with Lime Slice

Sparkling Mineral Water

HELPFUL HINTS: *Vary this week's recipe* by using 10 ounces of peeled, deveined shrimp or any firm-fleshed white fish like haddock or halibut instead of scallops. Out of vermouth and shallots? Use 2 tablespoons of white wine and 1 tablespoon of minced onion instead.

To keep scallops, cover loosely and store in the coldest section of the refrigerator. Use within 1 or 2 days.

Time-saving tip: Dredge foods on wax paper—you will have one less dish to wash.

A WORD FROM JEAN NIDETCH: Being "too tired to bother" preparing proper meals after an exhausting day can lead you to grab the wrong foods because it seems easier. To counter this pitfall, set aside one evening or part of the weekend to prepare and freeze a week's meals, ready for easy warming-up. Don't forget you can get twice as much mileage from your efforts by cooking double amounts and freezing for the future, not just the week.

PLAN FOR SUCCESS

What I succeeded at this week _____

_____

Goal for next week _____

Sautéed Scallops Provençale

Makes 2 servings

As with most other types of seafood, scallops are quick-cooking, the perfect food for busy cooks.

10 ounces scallops (fresh or frozen)
1 tablespoon plus 1½ teaspoons all-purpose flour
⅛ teaspoon each salt and pepper
1 tablespoon each olive oil and minced shallots
½ garlic clove, minced
1 medium tomato, blanched, peeled, seeded, and chopped
2 tablespoons dry vermouth
1 teaspoon chopped fresh basil or ¼ teaspoon dried
Garnish: chopped fresh Italian parsley

Rinse scallops in cold water and, using paper towels, pat dry; if scallops are large, cut into bite-size pieces. On sheet of wax paper, or on paper plate, combine flour, salt, and pepper; dredge scallops in flour mixture, coating all sides and using all of mixture.

In 9-inch nonstick skillet heat oil; add shallots and garlic and sauté for about 30 seconds. Add scallops and cook, stirring constantly, until lightly browned, about 3 minutes. Add remaining ingredients except garnish and cook for 3 minutes longer; serve sprinkled with parsley.

Each serving provides: 4 Protein Exchanges; 1 Vegetable Exchange; 1½ Fat Exchanges; 40 calories Optional Exchange

Per serving: 235 calories, 23 g protein, 8 g fat, 14 g carbohydrate, 504 mg sodium, 50 mg cholesterol

WEEKLY FOOD DIARY

	MONDAY	TUESDAY	WEDNESDAY	THURSDAY	FRIDAY	SATURDAY	SUNDAY
BREAKFAST FRUIT PROTEIN BREAD FAT MILK OPTIONAL							
LUNCH PROTEIN BREAD VEGETABLES FAT FRUIT MILK OPTIONAL							
DINNER PROTEIN BREAD VEGETABLES FAT FRUIT MILK OPTIONAL							
SNACKS							
DAILY CHECK LIST FRUIT VEG. MILK BREAD FAT PROTEIN OPTIONAL CALORIES							

WEEKLY CHECKLIST OF LIMITED PROTEIN EXCHANGES

EGGS ◯◯◯◯   MEAT GROUP ◯◯◯◯◯◯◯◯◯◯◯◯

SEMISOFT OR HARD CHEESE ◯◯◯   LIVER ◯◯◯◯◯◯

COMMENTS:

ENGAGEMENTS

JUNE

1985

MONDAY
10

TUESDAY
11

WEDNESDAY
12

THURSDAY
13

Flag Day

FRIDAY
14

SATURDAY
15

Father's Day

SUNDAY
16

	S	M	T	W	T	F	S
MAY				1	2	3	4
	5	6	7	8	9	10	11
	12	13	14	15	16	17	18
	19	20	21	22	23	24	25
	26	27	28	29	30	31	

	S	M	T	W	T	F	S
JUNE							1
	2	3	4	5	6	7	8
	9	10	11	12	13	14	15
	16	17	18	19	20	21	22
	23	24	25	26	27	28	29
	30						

	S	M	T	W	T	F	S
JULY		1	2	3	4	5	6
	7	8	9	10	11	12	13
	14	15	16	17	18	19	20
	21	22	23	24	25	26	27
	28	29	30	31			

W E I G H T

MENU

W A T C H E R S

Deviled Eggs

Cucumber-Cheese Salad

Sesame Melba Rounds

Apricots

Iced Coffee or Tea

HELPFUL HINTS: *For good salads,* make sure all ingredients are thoroughly dry. Water will dilute the dressing and keep it from clinging.

Time-saving tips: (1) Make dressing and salad separately early in the day. (2) Use seedless cucumbers to save a step in preparation. (3) Instead of making deviled eggs, dice 2 hard-cooked eggs and add to the salad.

A WORD FROM JEAN NIDETCH: Instead of flagging "Stop" signals at yourself, set up some "Go" signs that point to sights more rewarding than food. For instance, when you have a lonely evening ahead of you, ordering yourself not to go near the kitchen just sets up "kitchen" as a mental magnet! It's safer to arrange some pleasant *options;* like promising yourself to make a long-distance call to a friend, or treating yourself to a new mystery that will make the evening enjoyable. This gives you a healthy outlook on what you're *getting,* rather than what you're *not*—and it staves off a "poor me" refrigerator raid.

PLAN FOR SUCCESS

What I succeeded at this week _____

_____

Goal for next week _____

Cucumber-Cheese Salad

Makes 2 servings

2 chilled medium cucumbers
4 ounces Muenster cheese, cut into thin
    strips
1 cup julienne-cut chilled red bell pepper
    (thin strips)
½ cup each sliced chilled celery and
    scallions (green onions)
½ cup plain low-fat yogurt
1 tablespoon rice vinegar
1 teaspoon each Dijon-style mustard and
    prepared horseradish
½ teaspoon Worcestershire sauce
¼ teaspoon each salt and pepper

Pare cucumbers and cut into halves lengthwise; using the tip of a teaspoon, scoop out and discard seeds. Cut cucumbers into ¼-inch-thick slices.

In salad bowl combine cucumbers, cheese, red pepper, celery, and scallions. In small bowl combine remaining ingredients, mixing well; pour over vegetable mixture and toss to combine.

Each serving provides: 2 Protein Exchanges; 4 Vegetable Exchanges; ½ Milk Exchange
Per serving: 307 calories, 19 g protein, 19 g fat, 19 g carbohydrate, 811 mg sodium, 58 mg cholesterol

WEEKLY FOOD DIARY

	MONDAY	TUESDAY	WEDNESDAY	THURSDAY	FRIDAY	SATURDAY	SUNDAY
BREAKFAST FRUIT PROTEIN BREAD FAT MILK OPTIONAL							
LUNCH PROTEIN BREAD VEGETABLES FAT FRUIT MILK OPTIONAL							
DINNER PROTEIN BREAD VEGETABLES FAT FRUIT MILK OPTIONAL							
SNACKS							
DAILY CHECK LIST FRUIT VEG. MILK BREAD FAT PROTEIN OPTIONAL	○○○ ○○○ ○○ ○○○ ○○ ○○○○○○○ ☐ CALORIES	○○○ ○○○ ○○ ○○○ ○○ ○○○○○○○ ☐ CALORIES	○○○ ○○○ ○○ ○○○ ○○ ○○○○○○○ ☐ CALORIES	○○○ ○○○ ○○ ○○○ ○○ ○○○○○○○ ☐ CALORIES	○○○ ○○○ ○○ ○○○ ○○ ○○○○○○○ ☐ CALORIES	○○○ ○○○ ○○ ○○○ ○○ ○○○○○○○ ☐ CALORIES	○○○ ○○○ ○○ ○○○ ○○ ○○○○○○○ ☐ CALORIES

WEEKLY CHECKLIST OF LIMITED PROTEIN EXCHANGES

EGGS ○○○ ○○○   MEAT GROUP ○○○○○○○○

SEMISOFT OR ○○○ ○○○   LIVER ○○○○
HARD CHEESE

COMMENTS:

JUNE

MONDAY
17

TUESDAY
18

WEDNESDAY
19

THURSDAY
20

FRIDAY
21

SATURDAY
22

SUNDAY
23

	S	M	T	W	T	F	S
MAY				1	2	3	4
	5	6	7	8	9	10	11
	12	13	14	15	16	17	18
	19	20	21	22	23	24	25
	26	27	28	29	30	31	

	S	M	T	W	T	F	S
JUNE							1
	2	3	4	5	6	7	8
	9	10	11	12	13	14	15
	16	17	18	19	20	21	22
	23	24	25	26	27	28	29
	30						

	S	M	T	W	T	F	S
JULY		1	2	3	4	5	6
	7	8	9	10	11	12	13
	14	15	16	17	18	19	20
	21	22	23	24	25	26	27
	28	29	30	31			

Broiled Fish with Lemon Slices

Corn on the Cob

Steamed Green Beans

Cherry Tomatoes, Sliced Celery, and
Torn Lettuce with Italian Dressing

Frozen Strawberry Yogurt

White Wine Spritzer

HELPFUL HINTS: *To vary the recipe*, use 2 cups of blueberries instead of the strawberries (and double the Fruit Exchange).

To make superfine sugar, process granulated sugar in the blender or food processor.

Cooking tips for fish: Allow about 10 minutes of cooking time per inch of thickness for fresh or thawed frozen fish, and about 20 minutes for unthawed frozen fish. (You needn't defrost frozen fish unless the recipe specifies it.) Fish is done when it is opaque and flakes easily when tested with a fork.

A WORD FROM JEAN NIDETCH: If the dinner table seems like an obstacle course, here are a couple of useful tips. *When it comes to "seconds," put your needs first.* Don't put platters of extra helpings on the table. Place them out of your reach, and tell people to serve themselves. *Remember that less looks like more when it's on a smaller plate.* "A smaller plate equals a smaller size" is a good motto to remember.

PLAN FOR SUCCESS

What I succeeded at this week _____

_____

Goal for next week _____

Frozen Strawberry Yogurt

Makes 4 servings

2 cups strawberries, sliced
1 cup plain low-fat yogurt
1 tablespoon superfine sugar

In blender container or work bowl of food processor puree strawberries; if desired, press through sieve to remove seeds. In bowl combine fruit, yogurt, and sugar; pour into 2-quart freezer container, cover, and freeze until mixture becomes slightly thickened, about 30 minutes.

Remove container from freezer and stir mixture vigorously to break up ice particles; cover and return to freezer. Repeat stirring procedure every 15 to 20 minutes until mixture resembles soft sherbet (if mixture hardens, it can be softened by processing in food processor). Serve immediately or freeze for future use.

Each serving provides: ½ Fruit Exchange; ½ Milk Exchange; 15 calories Optional Exchange
Per serving: 70 calories, 3 g protein, 1 g fat, 12 g carbohydrate, 40 mg sodium, 3 mg cholesterol

WEEKLY FOOD DIARY

	MONDAY	TUESDAY	WEDNESDAY	THURSDAY	FRIDAY	SATURDAY	SUNDAY
BREAKFAST FRUIT PROTEIN BREAD FAT MILK OPTIONAL							
LUNCH PROTEIN BREAD VEGETABLES FAT FRUIT MILK OPTIONAL							
DINNER PROTEIN BREAD VEGETABLES FAT FRUIT MILK OPTIONAL							
SNACKS							

DAILY CHECK LIST

FRUIT
VEG.
MILK
BREAD
FAT
PROTEIN
OPTIONAL

CALORIES (Monday, Tuesday, Wednesday, Thursday, Friday, Saturday, Sunday)

WEEKLY CHECKLIST OF LIMITED PROTEIN EXCHANGES

EGGS

SEMISOFT OR
HARD CHEESE

MEAT GROUP

LIVER

COMMENTS:

JUNE

1985

MONDAY
24

TUESDAY
25

WEDNESDAY
26

THURSDAY
27

FRIDAY
28

SATURDAY
29

SUNDAY
30

	S	M	T	W	T	F	S
				1	2	3	4
M	5	6	7	8	9	10	11
A	12	13	14	15	16	17	18
Y	19	20	21	22	23	24	25
	26	27	28	29	30	31	

	S	M	T	W	T	F	S
							1
J	2	3	4	5	6	7	8
U	9	10	11	12	13	14	15
N	16	17	18	19	20	21	22
E	23	24	25	26	27	28	29
	30						

	S	M	T	W	T	F	S
		1	2	3	4	5	6
J	7	8	9	10	11	12	13
U	14	15	16	17	18	19	20
L	21	22	23	24	25	26	27
Y	28	29	30	31			

Beef Kabobs

Brown Rice with Chopped Chives and Parsley

Romaine and Red Onion Salad with
Herb Vinaigrette Dressing

Watermelon

Lemonade

HELPFUL HINTS: *Vary this week's recipe* by substituting cubed skinned chicken, lamb, or veal for the beef; use 1 red or green bell pepper cut into squares in place of the mushroom caps.

Cooking tips: Before cubing meat, place it in the freezer until just firm to make cutting easier. If wooden skewers are used, soak them in water before using to prevent burning.

A WORD FROM JEAN NIDETCH: Draw up your Declaration of Independence from food "pushers." "I made it just for you," wails your mother (sister, cousin, friend). Chances are she made it to satisfy her ego needs. Keeping in mind *your* growing ego (and shrinking shape), counter with: "You always make foods look so lovely. I *admire* it, but I just can't *eat* it." You've staved off the calories, while deftly feeding her a compliment. And develop some glib party lines for hosts who push hors d'oeuvres your way; like a simple, "Later." (Who has to know that "later" may mean a goal year from now?)

PLAN FOR SUCCESS

What I succeeded at this week _____

_____

Goal for next week _____

Beef Kabobs

Makes 4 servings, 2 skewers each

Sauce

3 tablespoons barbecue sauce
2 tablespoons plus 2 teaspoons reduced-calorie
     orange marmalade (16 calories per 2 teaspoons)
1 tablespoon plus 1 teaspoon teriyaki sauce
Water

Kabobs

10 ounces cubed beef tenderloin or sirloin
     (about 1-inch cubes)
16 cherry tomatoes
16 small mushroom caps (about 1-inch diameter
     each)

To Prepare Sauce: In small mixing bowl combine barbecue sauce with marmalade and teriyaki sauce; stir in enough water to blend mixture to spreading consistency (no more than 2 tablespoons) and mix thoroughly.

To Prepare Kabobs: Onto each of eight 12-inch skewers thread ⅛ of the beef, 2 cherry tomatoes, and 2 mushroom caps, alternating ingredients. On rack in broiling pan broil kabobs until meat is browned on top; turn skewers over and broil, basting frequently with sauce, just until other side of meat is browned (do not overcook or tomatoes will split).* Serve with any remaining sauce that has not been used for basting.

*Kabobs can also be grilled outdoors, on rack over hot coals.

Each serving provides: 2 Protein Exchanges; 1 Vegetable Exchange; 30 calories Optional Exchange
Per serving: 171 calories, 20 g protein, 5 g fat, 12 g carbohydrate, 394 mg sodium, 52 mg cholesterol

WEEKLY FOOD DIARY

	MONDAY	TUESDAY	WEDNESDAY	THURSDAY	FRIDAY	SATURDAY	SUNDAY
BREAKFAST FRUIT PROTEIN BREAD FAT MILK OPTIONAL							
LUNCH PROTEIN BREAD VEGETABLES FAT FRUIT MILK OPTIONAL							
DINNER PROTEIN BREAD VEGETABLES FAT FRUIT MILK OPTIONAL							
SNACKS							
DAILY CHECK LIST FRUIT VEG. MILK BREAD FAT PROTEIN OPTIONAL	CALORIES	CALORIES	CALORIES	CALORIES	CALORIES	CALORIES	CALORIES

WEEKLY CHECKLIST OF LIMITED PROTEIN EXCHANGES

EGGS ○○○○
SEMISOFT OR HARD CHEESE ○○○○
MEAT GROUP ○○○○○○○○
LIVER ○○○○

COMMENTS:

JULY

1 9 8 5

Canada Day (Canada)

MONDAY
1

TUESDAY
2

WEDNESDAY
3

Independence Day

THURSDAY
4

FRIDAY
5

SATURDAY
6

SUNDAY
7

	S	M	T	W	T	F	S
							1
J	2	3	4	5	6	7	8
U	9	10	11	12	13	14	15
N	16	17	18	19	20	21	22
E	23	24	25	26	27	28	29
	30						

	S	M	T	W	T	F	S
		1	2	3	4	5	6
J	7	8	9	10	11	12	13
U	14	15	16	17	18	19	20
L	21	22	23	24	25	26	27
Y	28	29	30	31			

	S	M	T	W	T	F	S
					1	2	3
A	4	5	6	7	8	9	10
U	11	12	13	14	15	16	17
G	18	19	20	21	22	23	24
	25	26	27	28	29	30	31

WEIGHT

MENU

WATCHERS

Broiled or Sautéed Chicken Livers

Broad Noodles with Poppy Seed

Seasoned Green Beans

Fruit Salad

Iced Coffee or Tea

HELPFUL HINTS: *For a hot-weather dish,* chill Seasoned Green Beans before serving. The combination of seasonings in the recipe also goes well with tomatoes, zucchini, carrots, and eggplant.

Time-saving tip: Keep cut-up onion and garlic on hand in covered containers in the refrigerator; they will keep for about a week.

For cubes that won't dilute iced coffee or tea, freeze coffee or tea in ice cube trays and use cubes to chill the beverage.

A WORD FROM JEAN NIDETCH: A vacation by car needn't drive you into a detour. Invest in a cooler and stock it with "first aids" to avoid being trapped into grabbing anything at fast-food stops. You can replenish your supplies from roadside fruit and vegetable stands. By adding other "bring-alongs," such as coffee, tea, bouillon, unsweetened cocoa, or nonfat dry milk, you can have a safe pick-me-up, either hot or chilled. And take advantage of every chance for exercise, including motel pools.

PLAN FOR SUCCESS

What I succeeded at this week _____

_____

Goal for next week _____

Seasoned Green Beans

Makes 4 servings

40 whole flat green beans, trimmed
    (10 to 11 ounces untrimmed)
2 cups water
1 tablespoon plus 1 teaspoon margarine
¼ cup diced onion
1 garlic clove, minced
2 tablespoons chopped fresh parsley
2 teaspoons chopped fresh basil
¼ teaspoon each salt and crushed
    rosemary leaves

In 1-quart saucepan cook green beans in water until tender. Drain beans; transfer to heatproof bowl, set aside, and keep warm.

In small nonstick skillet heat margarine until bubbly and hot; add onion and garlic and sauté until onion is translucent. Stir in remaining ingredients except beans and cook for 1 minute longer. Pour onion mixture over cooked beans; toss well to coat and serve immediately.

Each serving provides: 2 Vegetable Exchanges; 1 Fat Exchange

Per serving: 61 calories, 2 g protein, 4 g fat, 6 g carbohydrate, 185 mg sodium, 0 mg cholesterol

WEEKLY FOOD DIARY

	MONDAY	TUESDAY	WEDNESDAY	THURSDAY	FRIDAY	SATURDAY	SUNDAY
BREAKFAST FRUIT PROTEIN BREAD FAT MILK OPTIONAL							
LUNCH PROTEIN BREAD VEGETABLES FAT FRUIT MILK OPTIONAL							
DINNER PROTEIN BREAD VEGETABLES FAT FRUIT MILK OPTIONAL							
SNACKS							
DAILY CHECK LIST FRUIT VEG. MILK BREAD FAT PROTEIN OPTIONAL CALORIES	○○○○○○○ CALORIES	○○○○○○○ CALORIES	○○○○○○○ CALORIES	○○○○○○○ CALORIES	○○○○○○○ CALORIES	○○○○○○○ CALORIES	○○○○○○○ CALORIES

WEEKLY CHECKLIST OF LIMITED PROTEIN EXCHANGES

EGGS ○○○

SEMISOFT OR ○○○
HARD CHEESE

MEAT GROUP ○○○○○○○○○○

LIVER ○○○

COMMENTS:

JULY

1 9 8 5

MONDAY
8

TUESDAY
9

WEDNESDAY
10

THURSDAY
11

FRIDAY
12

SATURDAY
13

SUNDAY
14

	S	M	T	W	T	F	S
J							1
U	2	3	4	5	6	7	8
N	9	10	11	12	13	14	15
E	16	17	18	19	20	21	22
	23	24	25	26	27	28	29
	30						

	S	M	T	W	T	F	S
J		1	2	3	4	5	6
U	7	8	9	10	11	12	13
L	14	15	16	17	18	19	20
Y	21	22	23	24	25	26	27
	28	29	30	31			

	S	M	T	W	T	F	S
A					1	2	3
U	4	5	6	7	8	9	10
G	11	12	13	14	15	16	17
	18	19	20	21	22	23	24
	25	26	27	28	29	30	31

WEIGHT MENU WATCHERS

Chilled Tomato Juice with
Celery Stick Stirrer

Caesar Chicken Salad

Italian Breadsticks

Melon Balls with Mint Sprig

Sparkling Mineral Water with
Lime Wedge

HELPFUL HINTS: *To vary the recipe,* use leftover cooked turkey or veal. Create a meatless version by using 1 cup cooked elbow macaroni or small shells instead of the chicken. (If you make this substitution, omit Protein Exchange and add 1 Bread Exchange to Exchange Information.)

Preparation tip: Use kitchen shears to dice the chicken, pimientos, and scallions.

A WORD FROM JEAN NIDETCH: Plan picnic menus as carefully as those for indoor meals. Hamburgers, franks, and chicken make barbecue life easy, but did you know that chicken *livers* make great grilling, too? Concoct deliciously filling salads from fresh vegetables in season. And reward your efforts with refreshing desserts of summertime fruits like watermelon. To help keep losing weight a "picnic," don't pack foods you are trying to avoid in the cooler where you might be tempted. If the children are having these foods, ask them to stay out of your line of vision.

PLAN FOR SUCCESS

What I succeeded at this week _____

_____

Goal for next week _____

Caesar Chicken Salad

Makes 2 servings

½ garlic clove
2 tablespoons plus 2 teaspoons lemon juice
1 tablespoon plus 1 teaspoon mayonnaise
2 teaspoons grated Parmesan cheese
8 ounces skinned and boned cooked chicken,
    chilled and diced
½ cup diced chilled celery
2 tablespoons diced drained canned pimientos
2 tablespoons chopped scallion (green onion)
4 pitted black olives, sliced
⅛ teaspoon each salt and pepper
4 chilled iceberg or romaine lettuce leaves

Rub a medium wooden bowl with cut side of garlic clove and discard garlic; add lemon juice, mayonnaise, and cheese to bowl and stir to combine. Add remaining ingredients except lettuce and mix well; line serving platter with lettuce and top with chicken mixture.

Each serving provides: 4 Protein Exchanges; 1¼ Vegetable Exchanges; 2 Fat Exchanges; 20 calories Optional Exchange

Per serving: 324 calories, 34 g protein, 18 g fat, 5 g carbohydrate, 429 mg sodium, 108 mg cholesterol

WEEKLY FOOD DIARY

	MONDAY	TUESDAY	WEDNESDAY	THURSDAY	FRIDAY	SATURDAY	SUNDAY
BREAKFAST FRUIT PROTEIN BREAD FAT MILK OPTIONAL							
LUNCH PROTEIN BREAD VEGETABLES FAT FRUIT MILK OPTIONAL							
DINNER PROTEIN BREAD VEGETABLES FAT FRUIT MILK OPTIONAL							
SNACKS							
DAILY CHECK LIST FRUIT VEG. MILK BREAD FAT PROTEIN OPTIONAL	CALORIES	CALORIES	CALORIES	CALORIES	CALORIES	CALORIES	CALORIES

WEEKLY CHECKLIST OF LIMITED PROTEIN EXCHANGES

EGGS ○○○○

SEMISOFT OR HARD CHEESE ○○○

MEAT GROUP ○○○○○○○○

LIVER ○○○

COMMENTS:

ENGAGEMENTS

JULY

1 9 8 5

MONDAY
15

TUESDAY
16

WEDNESDAY
17

THURSDAY
18

FRIDAY
19

SATURDAY
20

SUNDAY
21

JUNE	S	M	T	W	T	F	S
							1
	2	3	4	5	6	7	8
	9	10	11	12	13	14	15
	16	17	18	19	20	21	22
	23	24	25	26	27	28	29
	30						

JULY	S	M	T	W	T	F	S
		1	2	3	4	5	6
	7	8	9	10	11	12	13
	14	15	16	17	18	19	20
	21	22	23	24	25	26	27
	28	29	30	31			

AUG	S	M	T	W	T	F	S
					1	2	3
	4	5	6	7	8	9	10
	11	12	13	14	15	16	17
	18	19	20	21	22	23	24
	25	26	27	28	29	30	31

Broiled or Barbecued Lamb Chop with
Chopped Fresh Mint

Corn on the Cob with Margarine

Sliced Tomato and Mushroom Salad
with Reduced-Calorie French Dressing

Blueberry-Vanilla Parfait

Iced Tea with Lemon Wedge

HELPFUL HINTS: *Vary this week's recipe* by using 2 cups of strawberries or 2 medium fresh peaches (or 1 cup of canned sliced peaches—no sugar added) instead of the blueberries. Grape spread can complement any fruit you choose, as its flavor is neutral.

The fruit topping in this recipe is also good on dietary frozen dessert or hot cereal.

To keep lamb chops from curling, remove all visible fat and slash the edges before cooking.

A WORD FROM JEAN NIDETCH: The best way to stop round-the-clock nibbling is to plan your snacks for specific times, just as your meals are (or should be). No grabbing food on the run. Whether you're eating indoors or out, take time to sit down and enjoy your snack in a leisurely way. Use tricks to prolong the pleasure—for example, slice fruit instead of eating it whole. It seems to last longer that way. It's good eating form—and great for your form too.

PLAN FOR SUCCESS

What I succeeded at this week _____

_____

Goal for next week _____

Blueberry-Vanilla Parfait

Makes 4 servings

1 cup fresh blueberries (or frozen, no sugar added)
1 tablespoon plus 1 teaspoon reduced-calorie grape
    spread (16 calories per 2 teaspoons)
1½ teaspoons granulated sugar
1 teaspoon cornstarch, dissolved in 2 teaspoons water
2 cups skim milk
1 envelope (four ½-cup servings) reduced-calorie
    vanilla pudding mix

In blender container or work bowl of food processor puree blueberries; transfer puree to small saucepan and add grape spread and sugar. Bring to a boil; stir in dissolved cornstarch and cook, stirring constantly, until thickened. Let cool slightly, then cover and refrigerate until chilled.

In 1-quart saucepan combine milk and pudding mix and cook according to package directions; let cool just until thickened. Into each of four 6-ounce parfait glasses spoon ¼ of the pudding and ¼ of the puree, making alternate layers of each and ending with pudding; cover and refrigerate until set.

Each serving provides: ½ Fruit Exchange; 1 Milk Exchange; 20 calories Optional Exchange
Per serving: 124 calories, 5 g protein, 0.3 g fat, 26 g carbohydrate, 68 mg sodium, 2 mg cholesterol

WEEKLY FOOD DIARY

	MONDAY	TUESDAY	WEDNESDAY	THURSDAY	FRIDAY	SATURDAY	SUNDAY
BREAKFAST FRUIT PROTEIN BREAD FAT MILK OPTIONAL							
LUNCH PROTEIN BREAD VEGETABLES FAT FRUIT MILK OPTIONAL							
DINNER PROTEIN BREAD VEGETABLES FAT FRUIT MILK OPTIONAL							
SNACKS							
DAILY CHECK LIST FRUIT VEG. MILK BREAD FAT PROTEIN OPTIONAL	CALORIES	CALORIES	CALORIES	CALORIES	CALORIES	CALORIES	CALORIES

WEEKLY CHECKLIST OF LIMITED PROTEIN EXCHANGES

EGGS ○○○ ○○○

SEMISOFT OR
HARD CHEESE ○○○

MEAT GROUP ○○○○ ○○○○○

LIVER ○○○ ○○○

COMMENTS:

JULY

1 9 8 5

MONDAY
22

TUESDAY
23

WEDNESDAY
24

THURSDAY
25

FRIDAY
26

SATURDAY
27

SUNDAY
28

	S	M	T	W	T	F	S
JUNE							1
	2	3	4	5	6	7	8
	9	10	11	12	13	14	15
	16	17	18	19	20	21	22
	23	24	25	26	27	28	29
	30						

	S	M	T	W	T	F	S
JULY		1	2	3	4	5	6
	7	8	9	10	11	12	13
	14	15	16	17	18	19	20
	21	22	23	24	25	26	27
	28	29	30	31			

	S	M	T	W	T	F	S
AUG					1	2	3
	4	5	6	7	8	9	10
	11	12	13	14	15	16	17
	18	19	20	21	22	23	24
	25	26	27	28	29	30	31

Chilled Consommé with
Celery Stick Stirrer

Quick Spicy Veal 'n' Beans

Spinach and Sliced Radish Salad with
Reduced-Calorie Italian Dressing

Mango

Mineral Water with Lemon Twist

HELPFUL HINTS: *Vary this week's recipe* by substituting skinned chicken or turkey for the veal.

Some tips on chili powder: The secret of many Mexican dishes, this seasoning can add pep to scrambled eggs, omelets, soufflés, casseroles, ground meat dishes, or even hamburgers. As a change from garlic bread, make chili bread by blending chili powder with margarine; spread on bread and bake until golden.

A WORD FROM JEAN NIDETCH: If you're waiting for the blues to pass before starting some enjoyable activity, you've got the proverbial cart before the horse, for the way to change a mood is to *first change your actions, not the other way around*. It's also easier to alter your mental "scene" if the physical one becomes different. For instance, if you enjoy bicycling but are "too depressed to bother" until you feel better, try reversing emotional gears. Chances are you'll come back from your ride in a rosier frame of mind—and you won't have tried to *eat* your way out of the mood, either!

PLAN FOR SUCCESS

What I succeeded at this week _____

_____

Goal for next week _____

Quick Spicy Veal 'n' Beans

Makes 2 servings

2 teaspoons vegetable oil
½ cup each chopped onion and green
    bell pepper
1 teaspoon minced fresh garlic
8 ounces diced veal
1 teaspoon chili powder
½ teaspoon curry powder
Dash each salt and hot sauce
½ cup canned crushed tomatoes
1 tablespoon plus 1 teaspoon tomato
    paste
4 ounces drained canned pinto beans
1 cup cooked long-grain rice (hot)

In 1-quart saucepan heat oil; add onion, green pepper, and garlic and sauté until onion is translucent, about 5 minutes. Add veal and seasonings and cook until meat loses its pink color, about 3 minutes; add tomatoes and tomato paste and cook, stirring occasionally, for about 5 minutes. Add beans and cook until heated; serve over rice.

Each serving provides: 4 Protein Exchanges; 1 Bread Exchange; 1½ Vegetable Exchanges; 1 Fat Exchange; 10 calories Optional Exchange

Per serving: 458 calories, 32 g protein, 15 g fat, 49 g carbohydrate, 502 mg sodium (estimated), 86 mg cholesterol

WEEKLY FOOD DIARY

	MONDAY	TUESDAY	WEDNESDAY	THURSDAY	FRIDAY	SATURDAY	SUNDAY
BREAKFAST FRUIT PROTEIN BREAD FAT MILK OPTIONAL							
LUNCH PROTEIN BREAD VEGETABLES FAT FRUIT MILK OPTIONAL							
DINNER PROTEIN BREAD VEGETABLES FAT FRUIT MILK OPTIONAL							
SNACKS							
DAILY CHECK LIST FRUIT VEG. MILK BREAD FAT PROTEIN OPTIONAL CALORIES	○○○○○○○ ○○○○ ○○○○ ○○○ ○○○ ○○○○○○○ □ CALORIES	○○○○○○○ ○○○○ ○○○ ○○○ ○○○ ○○○○○○○ □ CALORIES	○○○○○○○ ○○○○ ○○○ ○○○ ○○○ ○○○○○○○ □ CALORIES	○○○○○○○ ○○○○ ○○○ ○○○ ○○○ ○○○○○○○ □ CALORIES	○○○○○○○ ○○○○ ○○○ ○○○ ○○○ ○○○○○○○ □ CALORIES	○○○○○○○ ○○○○ ○○○ ○○○ ○○○ ○○○○○○○ □ CALORIES	○○○○○○○ ○○○○ ○○○ ○○○ ○○○ ○○○○○○○ □ CALORIES

WEEKLY CHECKLIST OF LIMITED PROTEIN EXCHANGES

EGGS ○○○○ ○○○	MEAT GROUP ○○○○○○○ ○○○○○○○	
SEMISOFT OR HARD CHEESE ○○○○ ○○○	LIVER ○○○○	

COMMENTS:

JULY
AUGUST

1 9 8 5

MONDAY
29

TUESDAY
30

WEDNESDAY
31

THURSDAY
1

FRIDAY
2

SATURDAY
3

SUNDAY
4

	S	M	T	W	T	F	S
JUNE							1
	2	3	4	5	6	7	8
	9	10	11	12	13	14	15
	16	17	18	19	20	21	22
	23	24	25	26	27	28	29
	30						

	S	M	T	W	T	F	S
JULY		1	2	3	4	5	6
	7	8	9	10	11	12	13
	14	15	16	17	18	19	20
	21	22	23	24	25	26	27
	28	29	30	31			

	S	M	T	W	T	F	S
AUG					1	2	3
	4	5	6	7	8	9	10
	11	12	13	14	15	16	17
	18	19	20	21	22	23	24
	25	26	27	28	29	30	31

Grilled Ham and Cheese Sandwich

Chilled Sliced Beets

Carrot and Pickle Spears on Lettuce

Buttermilk-Orange Ice Pops

Coffee or Tea

HELPFUL HINTS: *To vary Buttermilk-Orange Ice Pops,* use 1 tablespoon plus 1 teaspoon of frozen concentrated pineapple or apple juice (with no sugar added) instead of the orange juice, and omit the orange peel.

Kitchen trick: To pare carrots and other vegetables efficiently, slide the blade of the vegetable peeler back and forth instead of in one direction.

A WORD FROM JEAN NIDETCH: Is nighttime eating turning your goal dream into a nightmare? Make midnight raids less dangerous by keeping a dish of salad-style vegetables in the refrigerator and restricting your reach to what's on that dish (not the ice cream in the freezer). Remember, too, that you'll be less likely to be awakened by genuine hunger if you save a snack for the late evening. Try not to mull over problems at bedtime, either. Reading or listening to soothing music before you go to bed is more apt to keep you dreaming (and dreamy).

PLAN FOR SUCCESS

What I succeeded at this week _____

_____

Goal for next week _____

Buttermilk-Orange Ice Pops

Makes 2 servings, 1 pop each

1 cup buttermilk
2 tablespoons thawed frozen concentrated
    orange juice (no sugar added)
1 teaspoon granulated sugar
¼ teaspoon grated orange peel

In small bowl combine all ingredients; mix well. Divide mixture into two 4- or 5- ounce plastic-coated paper cups; cover and freeze until partially frozen. Insert a wooden ice cream bar stick into each portion and freeze until completely frozen. To remove frozen pop from cup, use the point of a knife to loosen around edges, then unmold.

Each serving provides: ½ Fruit Exchange; ½ Milk Exchange; 25 calories Optional Exchange
Per serving: 87 calories, 5 g protein, 1 g fat, 15 g carbohydrate, 131 mg sodium, 5 mg cholesterol

WEEKLY FOOD DIARY

	MONDAY	TUESDAY	WEDNESDAY	THURSDAY	FRIDAY	SATURDAY	SUNDAY
BREAKFAST FRUIT PROTEIN BREAD FAT MILK OPTIONAL							
LUNCH PROTEIN BREAD VEGETABLES FAT FRUIT MILK OPTIONAL							
DINNER PROTEIN BREAD VEGETABLES FAT FRUIT MILK OPTIONAL							
SNACKS							

DAILY CHECK LIST

FRUIT
VEG.
MILK
BREAD
FAT
PROTEIN
OPTIONAL

CALORIES (each day)

WEEKLY CHECKLIST OF LIMITED PROTEIN EXCHANGES

EGGS ○○○○ ○○
SEMISOFT OR HARD CHEESE ○○○○ ○○

MEAT GROUP ○○○○○○ ○○○○○○○
LIVER ○○○○○○ ○○○○

COMMENTS:

AUGUST

1 9 8 5

MONDAY
5

TUESDAY
6

WEDNESDAY
7

THURSDAY
8

FRIDAY
9

SATURDAY
10

SUNDAY
11

	S	M	T	W	T	F	S
JULY		1	2	3	4	5	6
	7	8	9	10	11	12	13
	14	15	16	17	18	19	20
	21	22	23	24	25	26	27
	28	29	30	31			

	S	M	T	W	T	F	S
AUG					1	2	3
	4	5	6	7	8	9	10
	11	12	13	14	15	16	17
	18	19	20	21	22	23	24
	25	26	27	28	29	30	31

	S	M	T	W	T	F	S
SEPT	1	2	3	4	5	6	7
	8	9	10	11	12	13	14
	15	16	17	18	19	20	21
	22	23	24	25	26	27	28
	29	30					

B-B-Q Chicken

Baked Potato

Vegetable Medley in Foil

Coleslaw

Watermelon Wedge

Iced Coffee or Tea

HELPFUL HINTS: *To marinate chicken* or other foods, try using a self-sealing plastic bag. Place food in bag, then add marinade mixture and seal bag. Place in deep bowl; turn bag occasionally to distribute marinade evenly.

Time-saving tip: If you are barbecuing chicken, cook foil-wrapped vegetable medley on the grill at the same time. Try vegetables such as zucchini (and other summer squash), onions, bell peppers, eggplant, and tomatoes.

A WORD FROM JEAN NIDETCH: Plateau problems? They're a common part of the weight-loss story because your body needs time to adjust to change. It's helpful to keep a graph of your progress. You'll observe that although the line to goal doesn't go straight down but may tend to flatten out or even rise at times, the *overall* pattern is a downward one (assuming that you're staying on course). To keep your spirits up, keep track with a tape measure, too. Inches tend to come off even when the scale gets stubborn, especially if you do some exercise to help.

PLAN FOR SUCCESS

What I succeeded at this week _____

_____

Goal for next week _____

B-B-Q Chicken

Makes 4 servings

½ cup each chopped scallions (green onions) and tomato sauce
¼ cup each teriyaki sauce and spicy brown mustard
1 tablespoon plus 1 teaspoon cider vinegar
2 teaspoons each firmly packed brown sugar and molasses
2 garlic cloves, mashed
1¼ pounds skinned and boned chicken breasts
Garnish: parsley sprigs

In large glass or stainless steel bowl thoroughly combine all ingredients except chicken and garnish; add chicken, turning to coat. Cover and refrigerate for 1 hour, turning chicken again after about 30 minutes.

Spray barbecue grill with nonstick cooking spray. Cook chicken on grill over hot coals, turning several times and basting with marinade until chicken is tender and juices flow clear when chicken is pierced with a fork; serve garnished with parsley.

Each serving provides: 4 Protein Exchanges; ¾ Vegetable Exchange; 20 calories Optional Exchange
Per serving: 265 calories, 37 g protein, 6 g fat, 13 g carbohydrate, 986 mg sodium, 96 mg cholesterol

WEEKLY FOOD DIARY

	MONDAY	TUESDAY	WEDNESDAY	THURSDAY	FRIDAY	SATURDAY	SUNDAY
BREAKFAST FRUIT PROTEIN BREAD FAT MILK OPTIONAL							
LUNCH PROTEIN BREAD VEGETABLES FAT FRUIT MILK OPTIONAL							
DINNER PROTEIN BREAD VEGETABLES FAT FRUIT MILK OPTIONAL							
SNACKS							

DAILY CHECK LIST

FRUIT
VEG.
MILK
BREAD
FAT
PROTEIN
OPTIONAL

CALORIES   CALORIES   CALORIES   CALORIES   CALORIES   CALORIES   CALORIES

WEEKLY CHECKLIST OF LIMITED PROTEIN EXCHANGES

EGGS

MEAT GROUP

LIVER

SEMISOFT OR
HARD CHEESE

COMMENTS:

AUGUST

1 9 8 5

MONDAY
12

TUESDAY
13

WEDNESDAY
14

THURSDAY
15

FRIDAY
16

SATURDAY
17

SUNDAY
18

	S	M	T	W	T	F	S
JULY		1	2	3	4	5	6
	7	8	9	10	11	12	13
	14	15	16	17	18	19	20
	21	22	23	24	25	26	27
	28	29	30	31			

	S	M	T	W	T	F	S
AUG					1	2	3
	4	5	6	7	8	9	10
	11	12	13	14	15	16	17
	18	19	20	21	22	23	24
	25	26	27	28	29	30	31

	S	M	T	W	T	F	S
SEPT	1	2	3	4	5	6	7
	8	9	10	11	12	13	14
	15	16	17	18	19	20	21
	22	23	24	25	26	27	28
	29	30					

Sliced Chilled Roast Turkey with
Reduced-Calorie Russian Dressing

Pesto Potato Salad

Sliced Tomato and Cucumber on
Shredded Lettuce

Nectarine

Coffee or Tea

HELPFUL HINTS: *Keep pesto* (the basil dressing) on hand for use in soups, on broiled fish or steak, or over green beans or baked potato. Store in a jar with a tight-fitting cover and refrigerate for up to 2 weeks. Stir well before each use.

Use dressing to make pesto bread instead of garlic bread for an Italian dinner.

Cooking tip: Yogurt is a good substitute for mayonnaise and less expensive than sour cream; use it in place of either in recipes for sauces, soups, and salad dressings. It also combines well with fresh and canned fruits for a delicious dessert or snack.

A WORD FROM JEAN NIDETCH: "Putdown" is a term that generally doesn't have good associations, but there's one putdown you should make use of because it's helpful—the one that means putting down your fork or spoon in between each bite and letting it sit on the plate while you take time to taste, enjoy, and swallow. Not only will this make meals seem more satisfying, you'll have the time to discover what various foods *really* taste like.

PLAN FOR SUCCESS

What I succeeded at this week _____

_____

Goal for next week _____

Pesto Potato Salad

Makes 4 servings

This tasty salad goes well with hot or cold beef, veal, chicken, or turkey.

½ cup firmly packed fresh basil leaves
¼ cup plain low-fat yogurt
2 tablespoons each chopped fresh parsley and
    olive oil
1 tablespoon plus 1 teaspoon grated Parmesan
    cheese
1 medium garlic clove, minced
1 pound 2 ounces peeled boiled new potatoes,
    cut into quarters
2 cups cooked cut green beans (1-inch-long
    pieces)
¼ cup chopped drained canned pimientos
½ teaspoon salt

In blender container or work bowl of food processor combine first 5 ingredients and process until smooth—to make pesto.

In salad bowl combine remaining ingredients; pour dressing over potato mixture and toss well to coat. Cover and refrigerate until chilled.

Each serving provides: 1½ Bread Exchanges; 1⅛ Vegetable Exchanges; 1½ Fat Exchanges; 20 calories Optional Exchange

Per serving: 189 calories, 5 g protein, 8 g fat, 26 g carbohydrate, 318 mg sodium, 2 mg cholesterol

WEEKLY FOOD DIARY

	MONDAY	TUESDAY	WEDNESDAY	THURSDAY	FRIDAY	SATURDAY	SUNDAY
BREAKFAST FRUIT PROTEIN BREAD FAT MILK OPTIONAL							
LUNCH PROTEIN BREAD VEGETABLES FAT FRUIT MILK OPTIONAL							
DINNER PROTEIN BREAD VEGETABLES FAT FRUIT MILK OPTIONAL							
SNACKS							
DAILY CHECK LIST FRUIT VEG. MILK BREAD FAT PROTEIN OPTIONAL	○○○ ○○○ ○○○ ○○○ ○○○ ○○○ ○○○○○○ CALORIES ☐	○○○ ○○○ ○○○ ○○○ ○○○ ○○○ ○○○○○○ CALORIES ☐	○○○ ○○○ ○○○ ○○○ ○○○ ○○○ ○○○○○○ CALORIES ☐	○○○ ○○○ ○○○ ○○○ ○○○ ○○○ ○○○○○○ CALORIES ☐	○○○ ○○○ ○○○ ○○○ ○○○ ○○○ ○○○○○○ CALORIES ☐	○○○ ○○○ ○○○ ○○○ ○○○ ○○○ ○○○○○○ CALORIES ☐	○○○ ○○○ ○○○ ○○○ ○○○ ○○○ ○○○○○○ CALORIES ☐

WEEKLY CHECKLIST OF LIMITED PROTEIN EXCHANGES

EGGS ○○○○ MEAT GROUP ○○○○○○○○○○○○○○

SEMISOFT OR ○○○ LIVER ○○○○○○
HARD CHEESE

COMMENTS:

AUGUST

MONDAY
19

TUESDAY
20

WEDNESDAY
21

THURSDAY
22

FRIDAY
23

SATURDAY
24

SUNDAY
25

	S	M	T	W	T	F	S
JULY		1	2	3	4	5	6
	7	8	9	10	11	12	13
	14	15	16	17	18	19	20
	21	22	23	24	25	26	27
	28	29	30	31			

	S	M	T	W	T	F	S
AUG					1	2	3
	4	5	6	7	8	9	10
	11	12	13	14	15	16	17
	18	19	20	21	22	23	24
	25	26	27	28	29	30	31

	S	M	T	W	T	F	S
SEPT	1	2	3	4	5	6	7
	8	9	10	11	12	13	14
	15	16	17	18	19	20	21
	22	23	24	25	26	27	28
	29	30					

Rolled Sliced Chilled Roast Beef
with Horseradish-Yogurt Sauce

French Bread

Romaine Lettuce and Bean Sprout
Salad with Vinaigrette Dressing

Fresh Fruit Fondue

Espresso or Cappuccino

HELPFUL HINTS: *Vary the recipe* by using 4 medium peaches, pitted and sliced; 4 small nectarines, pitted and sliced; or 8 medium plums, pitted and sliced; or make any combinations you like in place of the strawberries and grapes.

To keep strawberries fresh, wash berries and remove caps just before using, not before storing. Washing removes the natural protective covering; the cap protects the berry and helps preserve flavor, texture, and nutrients.

A WORD FROM JEAN NIDETCH: The fortunate forecast is that you can trim pennies along with pounds. Keep an eye out for supermarket specials and stock up on nonperishables. Buy fresh produce economically when it's in season and investigate some less expensive varieties of fish and meat. Experiment with recipes that use meal-stretchers like legumes or those thrifty nutrition bargains, eggs and cheese. When you finally deduct from your food bills the money that isn't being wasted on "empty-calorie" junk foods, you'll be amazed. These figures will be reflected in the right amounts both in the budget and on the scale.

PLAN FOR SUCCESS

What I succeeded at this week _____

_____

Goal for next week _____

Fresh Fruit Fondue

Makes 8 servings

Fondues are fun for all. This delicious version is a wonderful indoor or outdoor dessert.

1 cup skim milk
1 envelope (two ½-cup servings) reduced-
    calorie custard mix
¼ cup thawed frozen dairy whipped topping
2 teaspoons freshly grated orange peel
2 cups strawberries
12 each large green and red seedless grapes

In saucepan heat milk to simmering point; add custard mix and cook, stirring constantly, until powder is dissolved. Remove from heat, cover, and refrigerate until slightly firm, about 30 minutes.

Fold whipped topping and orange peel into chilled custard and pour into a serving bowl; surround bowl with fresh fruit and use fondue forks or toothpicks to dip fruit into fondue.

Each serving provides: ½ Fruit Exchange; ¼ Milk Exchange; 5 calories Optional Exchange
Per serving: 52 calories, 2 g protein, 1 g fat, 11 g carbohydrate, 27 mg sodium, 0 mg cholesterol

WEEKLY FOOD DIARY

	MONDAY	TUESDAY	WEDNESDAY	THURSDAY	FRIDAY	SATURDAY	SUNDAY
BREAKFAST FRUIT PROTEIN BREAD FAT MILK OPTIONAL							
LUNCH PROTEIN BREAD VEGETABLES FAT FRUIT MILK OPTIONAL							
DINNER PROTEIN BREAD VEGETABLES FAT FRUIT MILK OPTIONAL							
SNACKS							
DAILY CHECK LIST FRUIT VEG. MILK BREAD FAT PROTEIN OPTIONAL	CALORIES	CALORIES	CALORIES	CALORIES	CALORIES	CALORIES	CALORIES

WEEKLY CHECKLIST OF LIMITED PROTEIN EXCHANGES

EGGS ○○○○

SEMISOFT OR HARD CHEESE ○○○

MEAT GROUP ○○○○○○○○○○

LIVER ○○○○○

COMMENTS:

ENGAGEMENTS

AUGUST
SEPTEMBER

1985

MONDAY
26

TUESDAY
27

WEDNESDAY
28

THURSDAY
29

FRIDAY
30

SATURDAY
31

SUNDAY
1

	S	M	T	W	T	F	S
JULY		1	2	3	4	5	6
	7	8	9	10	11	12	13
	14	15	16	17	18	19	20
	21	22	23	24	25	26	27
	28	29	30	31			

	S	M	T	W	T	F	S
AUG					1	2	3
	4	5	6	7	8	9	10
	11	12	13	14	15	16	17
	18	19	20	21	22	23	24
	25	26	27	28	29	30	31

	S	M	T	W	T	F	S
SEPT	1	2	3	4	5	6	7
	8	9	10	11	12	13	14
	15	16	17	18	19	20	21
	22	23	24	25	26	27	28
	29	30					

WEIGHT

MENU

WATCHERS

Barbecued Hamburger with Sautéed
Onions and Mushrooms in a Pita

Dill Pickle Chips

Tomato Relish

Honeydew and Cantaloupe Chunks

Iced Coffee or Tea

HELPFUL HINTS: *A versatile recipe,* Tomato Relish can be served as a refreshing starter to a meal, as a side dish, or as a tasty topping on cottage cheese.

Grow your own basil outside or indoors in a pot; it can be frozen or dried for year-round use. Just remember that dried herbs should generally be kept no longer than a year.

Time-saving tip: To shape hamburgers quickly, form ground meat into a cylinder, roll in plastic wrap, and freeze for about 1 hour; remove, unwrap, and cut meat into desired number of patties.

A WORD FROM JEAN NIDETCH: Celebrate Labor Day with a division of kitchen jobs. That's one way to avoid the "poor me" feeling that can sink in when you're faced with a load of dishes and the temptation of leftovers *to be put away*—not eaten by you. Ask for some company for physical and moral support. In union there is, indeed, strength.

PLAN FOR SUCCESS

What I succeeded at this week _____

_____

Goal for next week _____

Tomato Relish

Makes 4 servings

This is an excellent way to use your crop of home-grown tomatoes and basil.

2 medium tomatoes, finely diced
¼ cup each finely diced green bell
    pepper, celery, and onion
½ garlic clove, minced
2 teaspoons olive oil
1½ teaspoons chopped fresh basil
    or ½ teaspoon dried
½ teaspoon each salt, red wine
    vinegar, lemon juice, and honey
Dash each powdered mustard and pepper

In bowl combine all ingredients and toss thoroughly; cover and refrigerate until well chilled, about 2 hours.

Each serving provides: 1¼ Vegetable Exchanges; ½ Fat Exchange; 5 calories Optional Exchange
Per serving: 47 calories, 1 g protein, 3 g fat, 6 g carbohydrate, 283 mg sodium, 0 mg cholesterol

WEEKLY FOOD DIARY

	MONDAY	TUESDAY	WEDNESDAY	THURSDAY	FRIDAY	SATURDAY	SUNDAY
BREAKFAST FRUIT PROTEIN BREAD FAT MILK OPTIONAL							
LUNCH PROTEIN BREAD VEGETABLES FAT FRUIT MILK OPTIONAL							
DINNER PROTEIN BREAD VEGETABLES FAT FRUIT MILK OPTIONAL							
SNACKS							
DAILY CHECK LIST FRUIT VEG. MILK BREAD FAT PROTEIN OPTIONAL	○○○○ ○○○○ ○○○○ ○○○○○○○ CALORIES	○○○○ ○○○○ ○○○○ ○○○○○○○ CALORIES	○○○○ ○○○○ ○○○○ ○○○○○○○ CALORIES	○○○○ ○○○○ ○○○○ ○○○○○○○ CALORIES	○○○○ ○○○○ ○○○○ ○○○○○○○ CALORIES	○○○○ ○○○○ ○○○○ ○○○○○○○ CALORIES	○○○○ ○○○○ ○○○○ ○○○○○○○ CALORIES

WEEKLY CHECKLIST OF LIMITED PROTEIN EXCHANGES

EGGS ○○○○   MEAT GROUP ○○○○○○○○○○

SEMISOFT OR HARD CHEESE ○○○   LIVER ○○○

COMMENTS:

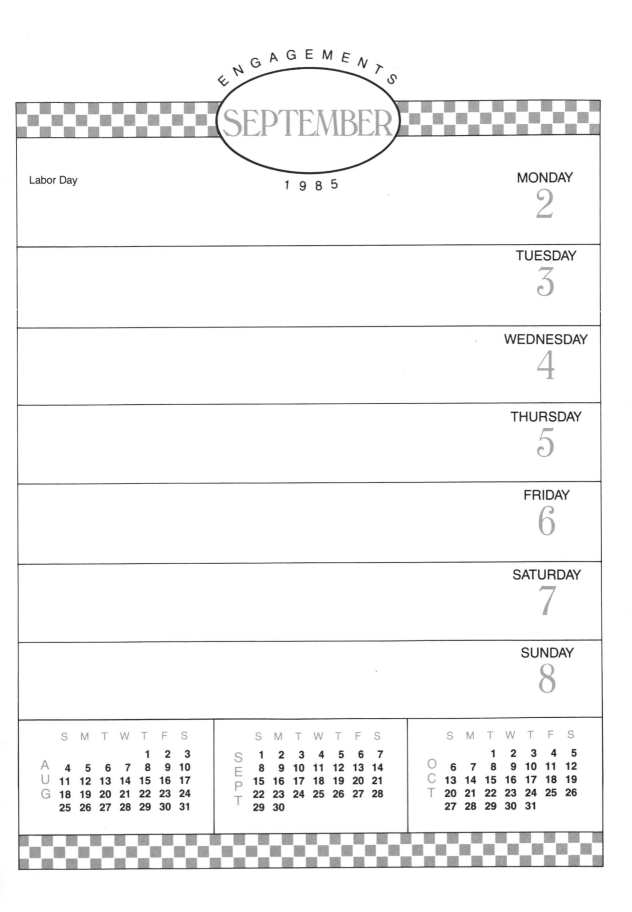

E N G A G E M E N T S

SEPTEMBER

1 9 8 5

Labor Day

MONDAY
2

TUESDAY
3

WEDNESDAY
4

THURSDAY
5

FRIDAY
6

SATURDAY
7

SUNDAY
8

	S	M	T	W	T	F	S
					1	2	3
A	4	5	6	7	8	9	10
U	11	12	13	14	15	16	17
G	18	19	20	21	22	23	24
	25	26	27	28	29	30	31

	S	M	T	W	T	F	S
S	1	2	3	4	5	6	7
E	8	9	10	11	12	13	14
P	15	16	17	18	19	20	21
T	22	23	24	25	26	27	28
	29	30					

	S	M	T	W	T	F	S
			1	2	3	4	5
O	6	7	8	9	10	11	12
C	13	14	15	16	17	18	19
T	20	21	22	23	24	25	26
	27	28	29	30	31		

Prosciutto and Peas Frittata

Sesame Breadsticks

Escarole and Chicory Salad
with Italian Dressing

Reduced-Calorie Chocolate Pudding
Sprinkled with Toasted Shredded Coconut

Coffee or Tea

HELPFUL HINTS: *Vary this week's recipe* by using a different kind of cheese and adding any chopped leftover vegetables you have on hand.

Tips on removing onion odors: To remove from a knife, run it through a raw potato. To remove from your hands, rub them briskly with celery salt before washing. To remove from your breath, eat parsley sprigs dipped in salt and vinegar.

To keep nonstick pans from scratching one another when stored stacked, place paper plates between them.

A WORD FROM JEAN NIDETCH: If you reward children or anyone else with "goodies," define your terms correctly. How "good" is a food that keeps you from looking your best? Train youngsters to value nutritious items like fruit as genuine "goodies." Have some *non*edible rewards, particularly the ones for yourself. Perhaps a pair of earrings to reward the ears that tuned out to "You must eat this." Or chic gloves for the hands that were so selective at the smorgasbord. Those are "goodies" worthy of the word.

PLAN FOR SUCCESS

What I succeeded at this week _____

_____

Goal for next week _____

Prosciutto and Peas Frittata

Makes 2 servngs

2 teaspoons margarine
¼ cup chopped onion
2 ounces prosciutto or boned
    "fully cooked" smoked ham, chopped
¼ cup drained canned or
    thawed frozen peas
2 large eggs
1 tablespoon water
Dash freshly ground pepper
2 ounces Swiss or Jarlsberg
    cheese, shredded

In small nonstick skillet that has a metal or removable handle heat margarine until bubbly and hot; add onion and sauté, stirring occasionally, until translucent, 3 to 4 minutes. Add prosciutto (or smoked ham) and cook over medium-high heat, stirring occasionally, for about 2 minutes; add peas and cook until heated through, stirring occasionally.

While peas are heating, in small bowl beat eggs with water and pepper; pour into skillet and stir quickly before eggs begin to set. Sprinkle with cheese and cook until bottom of frittata begins to set; transfer skillet to broiler and broil until frittata is puffed and lightly browned. Slide frittata onto a warmed serving platter.

Each serving provides: 3 Protein Exchanges; ¼ Vegetable Exchange; 1 Fat Exchange; 20 calories Optional Exchange

Per serving with canned peas: 339 calories, 22 g protein, 25 g fat, 7 g carbohydrate, 469 mg sodium, 325 mg cholesterol

With frozen peas: 336 calories, 22 protein, 25 g fat, 6 g carbohydrate, 447 mg sodium, 325 mg cholesterol

WEEKLY FOOD DIARY

	MONDAY	TUESDAY	WEDNESDAY	THURSDAY	FRIDAY	SATURDAY	SUNDAY
BREAKFAST FRUIT PROTEIN BREAD FAT MILK OPTIONAL							
LUNCH PROTEIN BREAD VEGETABLES FAT FRUIT MILK OPTIONAL							
DINNER PROTEIN BREAD VEGETABLES FAT FRUIT MILK OPTIONAL							
SNACKS							
DAILY CHECK LIST FRUIT VEG. MILK BREAD FAT PROTEIN OPTIONAL	☐ CALORIES	☐ CALORIES	☐ CALORIES	☐ CALORIES	☐ CALORIES	☐ CALORIES	☐ CALORIES

WEEKLY CHECKLIST OF LIMITED PROTEIN EXCHANGES

EGGS ○○○○

SEMISOFT OR ○○○
HARD CHEESE

MEAT GROUP ○○○○○○○○○

LIVER ○○○

COMMENTS:

ENGAGEMENTS

SEPTEMBER

1985

MONDAY
9

TUESDAY
10

WEDNESDAY
11

THURSDAY
12

FRIDAY
13

SATURDAY
14

SUNDAY
15

	S	M	T	W	T	F	S
						1	2	3
A	4	5	6	7	8	9	10
U	11	12	13	14	15	16	17
G	18	19	20	21	22	23	24
	25	26	27	28	29	30	31

	S	M	T	W	T	F	S
S	1	2	3	4	5	6	7
E	8	9	10	11	12	13	14
P	15	16	17	18	19	20	21
T	22	23	24	25	26	27	28
	29	30					

	S	M	T	W	T	F	S
			1	2	3	4	5
O	6	7	8	9	10	11	12
C	13	14	15	16	17	18	19
T	20	21	22	23	24	25	26
	27	28	29	30	31		

Lemony Sole Meunière

Barley with Sliced Mushrooms

Steamed Broccoli Spears

Stewed Fruit Compote

Coffee or Tea

HELPFUL HINTS: *To vary this week's recipe,* substitute scrod, snapper, or fresh salmon, or try shrimp.

A tip on lemons: Want just a little juice? Puncture the skin and gently squeeze out the amount needed. Want all you can get? Warm the lemon and roll it on a flat surface before squeezing.

Time-saving tip: Keep frozen mushrooms on hand, ready to use. To freeze, wash mushrooms and add to 1 quart boiling water seasoned with lemon juice and ½ teaspoon salt. Return to a boil. Cook for 3 minutes. Rinse in cold water, drain, pat dry, and seal in plastic freezer bags.

A WORD FROM JEAN NIDETCH: "How?" takes you further than "Why?" Asking yourself *why* things are bad ("Why do I always fall apart on weekends?") only leads to a dead-end street, unless followed by a question about *how* things can be changed. ("How can I plan ways to survive the weekends?") The answers will provide directional signals for moving forward.

PLAN FOR SUCCESS

What I succeeded at this week _____

_____

Goal for next week _____

Lemony Sole Meunière

Makes 2 servings

This is an excellent way to prepare any mild-flavored, delicate fish fillet.

2 tablespoons all-purpose flour
¼ teaspoon salt
Dash each pepper, onion powder, garlic powder,
     and paprika
2 sole fillets, 5 ounces each
1 tablespoon plus 1 teaspoon margarine
1 tablespoon each lemon juice and chopped
     fresh parsley
Garnish: lemon wedges and parsley sprigs

On sheet of wax paper thoroughly combine flour and seasonings; dredge fillets in mixture, coating evenly.

In 9-inch skillet heat margarine until bubbly and hot; add fish and cook over medium heat until browned on both sides. Sprinkle with lemon juice, then chopped parsley; serve garnished with lemon wedges and parsley sprigs.

Each serving provides: 4 Protein Exchanges; 2 Fat Exchanges; 30 calories Optional Exchange
Per serving: 212 calories, 25 g protein, 9 g fat, 7 g carbohydrate, 471 mg sodium, 71 mg cholesterol

WEEKLY FOOD DIARY

	MONDAY	TUESDAY	WEDNESDAY	THURSDAY	FRIDAY	SATURDAY	SUNDAY
BREAKFAST FRUIT PROTEIN BREAD FAT MILK OPTIONAL							
LUNCH PROTEIN BREAD VEGETABLES FAT FRUIT MILK OPTIONAL							
DINNER PROTEIN BREAD VEGETABLES FAT FRUIT MILK OPTIONAL							
SNACKS							

DAILY CHECK LIST

FRUIT
VEG.
MILK
BREAD
FAT
PROTEIN
OPTIONAL

CALORIES — CALORIES — CALORIES — CALORIES — CALORIES — CALORIES — CALORIES

WEEKLY CHECKLIST OF LIMITED PROTEIN EXCHANGES

EGGS ○○○○

MEAT GROUP ○○○○○○○○○○

SEMISOFT OR HARD CHEESE ○○○

LIVER ○○○○○

COMMENTS:

SEPTEMBER

1 9 8 5

Rosh Hashanah

MONDAY
16

TUESDAY
17

WEDNESDAY
18

THURSDAY
19

FRIDAY
20

SATURDAY
21

SUNDAY
22

	S	M	T	W	T	F	S
					1	2	3
A	4	5	6	7	8	9	10
U	11	12	13	14	15	16	17
G	18	19	20	21	22	23	24
	25	26	27	28	29	30	31

	S	M	T	W	T	F	S
S	1	2	3	4	5	6	7
E	8	9	10	11	12	13	14
P	15	16	17	18	19	20	21
T	22	23	24	25	26	27	28
	29	30					

	S	M	T	W	T	F	S
			1	2	3	4	5
O	6	7	8	9	10	11	12
C	13	14	15	16	17	18	19
T	20	21	22	23	24	25	26
	27	28	29	30	31		

Broiled Veal Chop

Cream-Style Corn

Cooked Asparagus Spears with
Margarine and Toasted Sesame Seed

Plum-Brandy Gelée

Cinnamon Coffee or Tea

HELPFUL HINTS: *To vary this week's recipe,* substitute 4 medium fresh peaches or 4 small fresh nectarines for the plums.

To toast sesame seeds, spread a thin layer in a skillet and toast, stirring constantly, over medium heat (or use a pan in a 350° F. oven) until seeds begin to change color, 5 to 6 minutes. Beware: they burn easily. Allow to cool. Transfer to airtight container. They will keep several weeks at room temperature, several months in the freezer.

A WORD FROM JEAN NIDETCH: Watch out for situations that you tend to pair with eating, even when you aren't hungry. Make a list of them so you can begin to be on guard. Next, cut out eating anywhere in the house but one designated spot—the dining room is safer than the kitchen. Then get rid of any habits like eating while reading or watching television. That way, turning on the TV won't turn on the "let's eat" channel.

PLAN FOR SUCCESS

What I succeeded at this week _____

_____

Goal for next week _____

Plum-Brandy Gelée

Makes 4 servings

8 medium sweet red plums, cut into halves
    and pitted
½ cup water, divided
2 envelopes unflavored gelatin
¼ cup granulated sugar
½ teaspoon vanilla extract
⅛ teaspoon grated lemon peel
Dash each ground cinnamon and brandy extract
¼ cup thawed frozen dairy whipped topping

In 1-quart saucepan combine plums with ¼ cup water; cover and cook over medium-low heat until very soft, 10 to 15 minutes.

Sprinkle gelatin over remaining ¼ cup water and let stand to soften.

Pour plums and cooking liquid into blender container and process until smooth; pour pureed fruit back into saucepan. Add sugar, vanilla, lemon peel, cinnamon, brandy extract, and softened gelatin; cook over low heat until sugar and gelatin are dissolved.

Divide plum mixture into 4 dessert dishes; cover and refrigerate until firm, about 4 hours. Serve each portion topped with 1 tablespoon whipped topping.

Each serving provides: 1 Fruit Exchange; 75 calories Optional Exchange
Per serving: 147 calories, 4 g protein, 2 g fat, 31 g carbohydrate, 3 mg sodium, 0 mg cholesterol

WEEKLY FOOD DIARY

	MONDAY	TUESDAY	WEDNESDAY	THURSDAY	FRIDAY	SATURDAY	SUNDAY
BREAKFAST FRUIT PROTEIN BREAD FAT MILK OPTIONAL							
LUNCH PROTEIN BREAD VEGETABLES FAT FRUIT MILK OPTIONAL							
DINNER PROTEIN BREAD VEGETABLES FAT FRUIT MILK OPTIONAL							
SNACKS							
DAILY CHECK LIST FRUIT VEG. MILK BREAD FAT PROTEIN OPTIONAL	○○○ ○○○ ○○○ ○○○○○○○ □ CALORIES	○○○ ○○○ ○○○○○○○ □ CALORIES	○○○ ○○○ ○○○○○○○ □ CALORIES	○○○ ○○○ ○○○○○○○ □ CALORIES	○○○ ○○○ ○○○○○○○ □ CALORIES	○○○ ○○○ ○○○○○○○ □ CALORIES	○○○ ○○○ ○○○○○○○ □ CALORIES

WEEKLY CHECKLIST OF LIMITED PROTEIN EXCHANGES

EGGS ○○○○

SEMISOFT OR HARD CHEESE ○○○

MEAT GROUP ○○○○○○○○○○○○

LIVER ○○○○○

COMMENTS:

MONDAY
23

TUESDAY
24

Yom Kippur

WEDNESDAY
25

THURSDAY
26

FRIDAY
27

SATURDAY
28

SUNDAY
29

	S	M	T	W	T	F	S
AUG					1	2	3
	4	5	6	7	8	9	10
	11	12	13	14	15	16	17
	18	19	20	21	22	23	24
	25	26	27	28	29	30	31

	S	M	T	W	T	F	S
SEPT	1	2	3	4	5	6	7
	8	9	10	11	12	13	14
	15	16	17	18	19	20	21
	22	23	24	25	26	27	28
	29	30					

	S	M	T	W	T	F	S
OCT			1	2	3	4	5
	6	7	8	9	10	11	12
	13	14	15	16	17	18	19
	20	21	22	23	24	25	26
	27	28	29	30	31		

W E I G H T

MENU

W A T C H E R S

Potato-Chard Soup

Broiled Chicken Breast

Parmesan-Topped Broiled Tomato

Steamed Chinese Pea Pods with
Bamboo Shoots

Pineapple Boat

White Wine

HELPFUL HINTS: *Served hot or chilled*, Potato-Chard Soup makes a good take-along lunch in an insulated vacuum container. You can substitute spinach for the chard.

Plan-ahead tip: Buy a whole chicken and cut into pieces. Broil the breast for this week's menu and save the leftovers to use for next week's recipe to make an extra-economical Quick Chicken 'n' Cannellini.

Seasoning tips: Try sprinkling chicken under the skin with garlic, thyme, paprika, lemon juice, white wine, chili powder, or curry powder. Remove and discard skin before serving.

A WORD FROM JEAN NIDETCH: Afraid that dinner invitation is going to sabotage your efforts? Why not phone your hostess for help. Ask for some simple substitutions to make things easier for you—and no harder for her. For instance, if something fried is on the menu, ask that your portion be broiled. And request that items like sour cream, butter, or gravy be sidelined from your servings. Suggest that one apple be left out of the pie, so you can savor the fruit in its natural state.

PLAN FOR SUCCESS

What I succeeded at this week _____

_____

Goal for next week _____

Potato-Chard Soup

Makes 4 servings

12 ounces peeled potatoes, sliced
2 cups water
2 cups chopped Swiss chard
½ cup chopped onion
2 packets instant chicken broth
 and seasoning mix
Dash each pepper and ground
 nutmeg (optional)

In 2-quart saucepan combine potatoes and water and bring to a boil. Reduce heat and let simmer for 10 minutes; add remaining ingredients and cook until vegetables are tender, about 15 minutes longer. Let soup cool, then pour half of mixture into blender container and process until smooth; transfer mixture to a bowl and process remaining soup until smooth. Pour soup back into saucepan and heat thoroughly.

Each serving provides: 1 Bread Exchange; 1¼ Vegetable Exchanges; 5 calories Optional Exchange
Per serving: 86 calories, 3 g protein, 0.2 g fat, 19 g carbohydrate, 468 mg sodium, 0 mg cholesterol

WEEKLY FOOD DIARY

	MONDAY	TUESDAY	WEDNESDAY	THURSDAY	FRIDAY	SATURDAY	SUNDAY
BREAKFAST FRUIT PROTEIN BREAD FAT MILK OPTIONAL							
LUNCH PROTEIN BREAD VEGETABLES FAT FRUIT MILK OPTIONAL							
DINNER PROTEIN BREAD VEGETABLES FAT FRUIT MILK OPTIONAL							
SNACKS							
DAILY CHECK LIST FRUIT VEG. MILK BREAD FAT PROTEIN OPTIONAL	○○○○ ○○○○ ○○○○ ○○○○ ○○○○○○○ □ CALORIES	○○○○ ○○○○ ○○○○ ○○○○ ○○○○○○○ □ CALORIES	○○○○ ○○○○ ○○○○ ○○○○ ○○○○○○○ □ CALORIES	○○○○ ○○○○ ○○○○ ○○○○ ○○○○○○○ □ CALORIES	○○○○ ○○○○ ○○○○ ○○○○ ○○○○○○○ □ CALORIES	○○○○ ○○○○ ○○○○ ○○○○ ○○○○○○○ □ CALORIES	○○○○ ○○○○ ○○○○ ○○○○ ○○○○○○○ □ CALORIES

WEEKLY CHECKLIST OF LIMITED PROTEIN EXCHANGES

EGGS ○○○ ○○○

SEMISOFT OR HARD CHEESE ○○○ ○○○

MEAT GROUP ○○○○○○○○○○○○○○

LIVER ○○○○○○

COMMENTS:

SEPTEMBER
OCTOBER

1985

MONDAY
30

TUESDAY
1

WEDNESDAY
2

THURSDAY
3

FRIDAY
4

SATURDAY
5

SUNDAY
6

	S	M	T	W	T	F	S
					1	2	3
AUG	4	5	6	7	8	9	10
	11	12	13	14	15	16	17
	18	19	20	21	22	23	24
	25	26	27	28	29	30	31

	S	M	T	W	T	F	S
	1	2	3	4	5	6	7
SEPT	8	9	10	11	12	13	14
	15	16	17	18	19	20	21
	22	23	24	25	26	27	28
	29	30					

	S	M	T	W	T	F	S
			1	2	3	4	5
OCT	6	7	8	9	10	11	12
	13	14	15	16	17	18	19
	20	21	22	23	24	25	26
	27	28	29	30	31		

Quick Skillet Chicken 'n' Cannellini

Elbow Macaroni

Lettuce and Tomato Salad with
Chopped Fresh Basil

Applesauce with Cinnamon

Sparkling Mineral Water

HELPFUL HINTS: *For a delicious meatless dish,* omit the chicken from this week's recipe. (Adjust Protein Exchange Information to 2 Exchanges.) Use red or pink beans if cannellini are not available.

Some salad tips: For iceberg lettuce so crisp it crackles, place in the freezer for a few minutes before serving. Or place a salad bowl of mixed greens in the freezer for a few minutes to crisp up. For whole lettuce leaves, core head and run cold water forcefully into the hole for 1 to 2 minutes. Clean leaves will separate easily.

A WORD FROM JEAN NIDETCH: Columbus Day reminds us that if we're going to set sail for a dream, we can't afford to let anyone talk us out of it. This means learning to turn a deaf ear to negative messages like "You're thin enough," when we haven't landed on goal yet. We have to learn to tune in to our own inner voice if we are to discover the new world that awaits each of us.

PLAN FOR SUCCESS

What I succeeded at this week _____

_____

Goal for next week _____

Quick Skillet Chicken 'n' Cannellini

Makes 2 servings

2 teaspoons all-purpose flour
Dash each salt and pepper
5 ounces skinned and boned chicken,
    cut into 1-inch cubes
2 teaspoons olive oil
½ cup each diced green bell
    pepper, onion, and celery
2 medium tomatoes, blanched, peeled,
    seeded, and chopped or 2 cups
    drained canned tomatoes, chopped
8 ounces drained canned white kidney
    beans (cannellini beans)
1 packet instant chicken broth and
    seasoning mix

On sheet of wax paper, or on a paper plate, combine flour, salt, and pepper; dredge chicken cubes in flour and set aside.

In 10-inch nonstick skillet heat oil over high heat; add chicken and brown on all sides (a few pieces at a time; do not crowd). Remove chicken from skillet and set aside.

To same skillet add green pepper, onion, and celery and cook over medium heat until vegetables are tender; add tomatoes and beans, sprinkle with broth mix, and stir to combine. Reduce heat to low, cover, and let simmer until mixture thickens, 5 to 8 minutes. Return chicken to skillet and stir to combine; cook, uncovered, until chicken is heated, about 5 minutes.

Each serving provides: 4 Protein Exchanges; 3½ Vegetable Exchanges; 1 Fat Exchange; 15 calories Optional Exchange

Per serving: 353 calories, 29 g protein, 10 g fat, 39 g carbohydrate, 965 mg sodium (estimated), 50 mg cholesterol

WEEKLY FOOD DIARY

DAILY CHECK LIST	MONDAY	TUESDAY	WEDNESDAY	THURSDAY	FRIDAY	SATURDAY	SUNDAY
BREAKFAST FRUIT PROTEIN BREAD FAT MILK OPTIONAL							
LUNCH PROTEIN BREAD VEGETABLES FAT FRUIT MILK OPTIONAL							
DINNER PROTEIN BREAD VEGETABLES FAT FRUIT MILK OPTIONAL							
SNACKS							
FRUIT VEG. MILK BREAD FAT PROTEIN OPTIONAL	CALORIES	CALORIES	CALORIES	CALORIES	CALORIES	CALORIES	CALORIES

WEEKLY CHECKLIST OF LIMITED PROTEIN EXCHANGES

EGGS ◯◯◯◯ ◯◯◯◯

SEMISOFT OR HARD CHEESE ◯◯◯ ◯◯◯

MEAT GROUP ◯◯◯◯◯◯ ◯◯◯◯◯◯

LIVER ◯◯◯ ◯◯◯

COMMENTS:

OCTOBER

1 9 8 5

MONDAY
7

TUESDAY
8

WEDNESDAY
9

THURSDAY
10

FRIDAY
11

Columbus Day

SATURDAY
12

SUNDAY
13

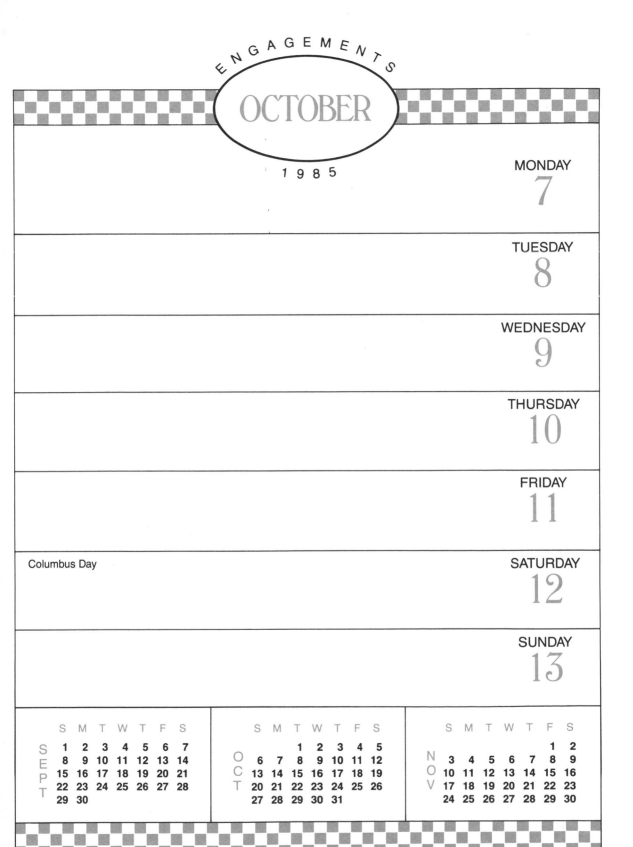

S	M	T	W	T	F	S
	1	2	3	4	5	6	7
SEPT	8	9	10	11	12	13	14
	15	16	17	18	19	20	21
	22	23	24	25	26	27	28
	29	30					

S	M	T	W	T	F	S
		1	2	3	4	5
OCT	6	7	8	9	10	11	12
	13	14	15	16	17	18	19
	20	21	22	23	24	25	26
	27	28	29	30	31		

S	M	T	W	T	F	S
						1	2
NOV	3	4	5	6	7	8	9
	10	11	12	13	14	15	16
	17	18	19	20	21	22	23
	24	25	26	27	28	29	30

Beef 'n' Cheddar Sauté

Broccoli Salad with Lemon Vinaigrette

Poached Pear Halves Topped with
Reduced-Calorie Strawberry Spread

Beer

HELPFUL HINTS: *Vary this week's recipe* by substituting leftover cooked ground chicken or veal for the beef and 1 cup of chopped carrots for the red or green pepper.

Time-saving tip: This hearty main dish is a good prepare-ahead recipe because its flavor is not hurt by reheating.

Economy tip: Don't let leftover tomato sauce go to waste. Pour it in measured amounts into ice cube trays. Once frozen, remove cubes and store, labeled, in plastic freezer bags.

A WORD FROM JEAN NIDETCH: The way to change a habit is to exchange it. For instance, when you come home, do you automatically head from the front door to the refrigerator door? Practice deliberately rerouting yourself in another direction, so that the first thing you do when you come home is switched to changing your clothes, making phone calls, or taking a relaxing bath. After a while, this new routine will be "automatic." As the old saying goes: "Habit is overcome by habit."

PLAN FOR SUCCESS

What I succeeded at this week _____

_____

Goal for next week _____

Beef 'n' Cheddar Sauté

Makes 4 servings

1 tablespoon plus 1 teaspoon vegetable oil
1 cup chopped onions
1 medium red or green bell pepper, seeded
    and chopped
1 garlic clove, minced
1 cup sliced mushrooms
12 ounces cooked ground beef, crumbled
½ cup tomato sauce
2 cups cooked small macaroni shells
4 ounces Cheddar cheese, shredded
¼ cup evaporated skimmed milk
2 teaspoons Worcestershire sauce
Dash each salt and pepper

In 12-inch skillet heat oil over medium heat; add onions, bell pepper, and garlic and sauté, stirring occasionally, for about 5 minutes. Add mushrooms and continue sautéing just until mushrooms begin to soften. Add beef and stir to break up any large pieces; add tomato sauce and bring to a boil. Reduce heat and let simmer to blend flavors, about 5 minutes. Add remaining ingredients and stir to combine; cook until heated through.

Each serving provides: 4 Protein Exchanges; 1 Bread Exchange; 2 Vegetable Exchanges; 1 Fat Exchange; 10 calories Optional Exchange

Per serving: 563 calories, 36 g protein, 34 g fat, 28 g carbohydrate, 469 mg sodium, 110 mg cholesterol

WEEKLY FOOD DIARY

	MONDAY	TUESDAY	WEDNESDAY	THURSDAY	FRIDAY	SATURDAY	SUNDAY
BREAKFAST FRUIT PROTEIN BREAD FAT MILK OPTIONAL							
LUNCH PROTEIN BREAD VEGETABLES FAT FRUIT MILK OPTIONAL							
DINNER PROTEIN BREAD VEGETABLES FAT FRUIT MILK OPTIONAL							
SNACKS							
DAILY CHECK LIST FRUIT VEG. MILK BREAD FAT PROTEIN OPTIONAL	○○○ ○○○ ○○○ ○○○ ○○○ ○○○ ○○○○○○ □ CALORIES	○○○ ○○○ ○○○ ○○○ ○○○ ○○○ ○○○○○○ □ CALORIES	○○○ ○○○ ○○○ ○○○ ○○○ ○○○ ○○○○○○ □ CALORIES	○○○ ○○○ ○○○ ○○○ ○○○ ○○○ ○○○○○○ □ CALORIES	○○○ ○○○ ○○○ ○○○ ○○○ ○○○ ○○○○○○ □ CALORIES	○○○ ○○○ ○○○ ○○○ ○○○ ○○○ ○○○○○○ □ CALORIES	○○○ ○○○ ○○○ ○○○ ○○○ ○○○ ○○○○○○ □ CALORIES

WEEKLY CHECKLIST OF LIMITED PROTEIN EXCHANGES

EGGS ○○○ ○○○

SEMISOFT OR HARD CHEESE ○○○ ○○○

MEAT GROUP ○○○○ ○○○○ ○○○○ ○○○○ ○○○○

LIVER ○○○○

COMMENTS:

ENGAGEMENTS

OCTOBER

Columbus Day (observed)
Thanksgiving Day (Canada)

1 9 8 5

MONDAY
14

TUESDAY
15

WEDNESDAY
16

THURSDAY
17

FRIDAY
18

SATURDAY
19

SUNDAY
20

S	M	T	W	T	F	S
S	**1**	**2**	**3**	**4**	**5**	**6**	**7**
E	**8**	**9**	**10**	**11**	**12**	**13**	**14**
P	**15**	**16**	**17**	**18**	**19**	**20**	**21**
T	**22**	**23**	**24**	**25**	**26**	**27**	**28**
	29	**30**					

S	M	T	W	T	F	S
		1	**2**	**3**	**4**	**5**
O	**6**	**7**	**8**	**9**	**10**	**11**	**12**
C	**13**	**14**	**15**	**16**	**17**	**18**	**19**
T	**20**	**21**	**22**	**23**	**24**	**25**	**26**
	27	**28**	**29**	**30**	**31**		

S	M	T	W	T	F	S
					1	**2**
N	**3**	**4**	**5**	**6**	**7**	**8**	**9**
O	**10**	**11**	**12**	**13**	**14**	**15**	**16**
V	**17**	**18**	**19**	**20**	**21**	**22**	**23**
	24	**25**	**26**	**27**	**28**	**29**	**30**

WEIGHT

MENU

WATCHERS

Cream of Cauliflower Soup

Poached Salmon Steak

Baked Potato Topped with
Plain Low-Fat Yogurt and Chopped Scallions

Steamed Sliced Carrots

Apple

HELPFUL HINTS: *Dress up soup* with a well-chosen garnish: grated cheese, imitation bacon bits, freshly chopped parsley or chives. Or serve it with carrot or celery sticks or cucumber slices.

For a uniformly baked potato, insert an aluminum or stainless-steel kitchen nail before baking. Never bake a potato without puncturing the skin—it can "explode."

A WORD FROM JEAN NIDETCH: Play Sherlock Holmes to unearth clues as to what may be injuring your weight-loss efforts. Keep hourly notes for the next few weeks, writing down the times when you remain on course—and when you go on little "detours." Be honest with yourself about every nibble. You'll soon discover which hours are problem times and can probably even see a pattern. Knowing *when* can help you understand the possible causes (lonely? bored? pressured?). Throwing a spotlight on the problems can help you do something about them.

PLAN FOR SUCCESS

What I succeeded at this week _____

_____

Goal for next week _____

Cream of Cauliflower Soup

Makes 2 servings

2 cups chopped cauliflower
1¾ cups water
2 packets instant chicken broth and
    seasoning mix
Dash white pepper
1 tablespoon margarine
2 tablespoons minced shallots or onion
2 teaspoons all-purpose flour
1 cup evaporated skimmed milk
2 tablespoons chopped fresh parsley

In 2-quart saucepan combine cauliflower, water, broth mix, and pepper; bring to a boil. Reduce heat to low and let simmer until cauliflower is tender, about 15 minutes. Transfer half of mixture to work bowl of food processor and puree; pour puree into a bowl and repeat procedure with remaining cauliflower mixture. Set aside.

In same saucepan heat margarine until bubbly and hot; add shallots (or onion) and sauté for about 30 seconds. Add flour and stir quickly to combine; using wire whisk, gradually stir in milk and continue cooking and stirring until mixture is thickened. Stir in cauliflower puree and cook until heated *(do not boil)*; serve immediately.

Each serving provides: 2 Vegetable Exchanges; 1½ Fat Exchanges; 1 Milk Exchange; 20 calories Optional Exchange

Per serving: 206 calories, 14 g protein, 6 g fat, 25 g carbohydrate, 1,062 mg sodium, 5 mg cholesterol

WEEKLY FOOD DIARY

	MONDAY	TUESDAY	WEDNESDAY	THURSDAY	FRIDAY	SATURDAY	SUNDAY
BREAKFAST FRUIT PROTEIN BREAD FAT MILK OPTIONAL							
LUNCH PROTEIN BREAD VEGETABLES FAT FRUIT MILK OPTIONAL							
DINNER PROTEIN BREAD VEGETABLES FAT FRUIT MILK OPTIONAL							
SNACKS							
DAILY CHECK LIST FRUIT VEG. MILK BREAD FAT PROTEIN OPTIONAL	○○○○ ○○○○ ○○○○ ○○○○○ ○○○ ○○○ □ CALORIES	○○○○ ○○○○ ○○○○ ○○○○○ ○○○ ○○○ □ CALORIES	○○○○ ○○○○ ○○○○ ○○○○○ ○○○ ○○○ □ CALORIES	○○○○ ○○○○ ○○○○ ○○○○○ ○○○ ○○○ □ CALORIES	○○○○ ○○○○ ○○○○ ○○○○○ ○○○ ○○○ □ CALORIES	○○○○ ○○○○ ○○○○ ○○○○○ ○○○ ○○○ □ CALORIES	○○○○ ○○○○ ○○○○ ○○○○○ ○○○ ○○○ □ CALORIES

WEEKLY CHECKLIST OF LIMITED PROTEIN EXCHANGES

EGGS ○○○○	MEAT GROUP ○○○○○○○○○○○○	
SEMISOFT OR HARD CHEESE ○○○ ○○○	LIVER ○○○○	

COMMENTS:

MONDAY
21

TUESDAY
22

WEDNESDAY
23

United Nations Day

THURSDAY
24

FRIDAY
25

SATURDAY
26

SUNDAY
27

	S	M	T	W	T	F	S
S		1	2	3	4	5	6	7
E		8	9	10	11	12	13	14
P		15	16	17	18	19	20	21
T		22	23	24	25	26	27	28
		29	30					

	S	M	T	W	T	F	S
O				1	2	3	4	5
C		6	7	8	9	10	11	12
T		13	14	15	16	17	18	19
		20	21	22	23	24	25	26
		27	28	29	30	31		

	S	M	T	W	T	F	S
N							1	2
O		3	4	5	6	7	8	9
V		10	11	12	13	14	15	16
		17	18	19	20	21	22	23
		24	25	26	27	28	29	30

Hamburger with Ketchup and Mustard

Sautéed Sliced Mushrooms

Red Onion Slices on Lettuce with
Oil and Vinegar Dressing

Maple-Glazed Popcorn Balls

Iced Tea with Lemon

HELPFUL HINTS: *Vary this week's recipe* by adding ¼ cup of raisins or 2 tea-spoons of sunflower seed or 1 tablespoon plus 1 teaspoon of shredded coconut. (Adjust Exchange Information accordingly.)

Store popcorn balls individually wrapped in plastic wrap in a cool, dry place.

For school or office lunch include a popcorn ball with a peanut butter and jelly sand-wich and an apple.

A WORD FROM JEAN NIDETCH: Don't let Halloween trick you out of treating yourself to goal. If you can't trust yourself to stay away from the trick-or-treat supplies, make sure that you stock nothing that can be your downfall. If need be, give your young callers coins instead of candies. And if your own children come home with treats, make a strict rule that they are to keep them to themselves, where you won't see them and be tempted. Taking these precautions will better your chance of looking bewitching.

PLAN FOR SUCCESS

What I succeeded at this week _____

_____

Goal for next week _____

Maple-Glazed Popcorn Balls

Makes 4 servings

A nutritious Halloween snack for your trick-or-treat visitors.

2 tablespoons each granulated
   sugar and light corn syrup
¼ teaspoon cider vinegar or
   white vinegar
1 teaspoon maple extract
4 cups prepared plain popcorn

In small nonstick saucepan combine sugar, syrup, and vinegar; stirring constantly, bring to a boil. Reduce heat and let simmer for about 2 minutes. Add extract and stir to combine; remove from heat.

Place popcorn in 2-quart flameproof bowl and place bowl on burner over *lowest* possible heat; add syrup mixture and toss gently until all popcorn is evenly coated. Wet hands slightly and shape and press popcorn mixture into 4 equal balls; let cool before serving.

Each serving provides: ½ Bread Exchange; 60 calories Optional Exchange
Per serving: 86 calories, 1 g protein, 0.4 g fat, 20 g carbohydrate, 7 mg sodium, 0 mg cholesterol

WEEKLY FOOD DIARY

	MONDAY	TUESDAY	WEDNESDAY	THURSDAY	FRIDAY	SATURDAY	SUNDAY
BREAKFAST FRUIT PROTEIN BREAD FAT MILK OPTIONAL							
LUNCH PROTEIN BREAD VEGETABLES FAT FRUIT MILK OPTIONAL							
DINNER PROTEIN BREAD VEGETABLES FAT FRUIT MILK OPTIONAL							
SNACKS							
DAILY CHECK LIST FRUIT VEG. MILK BREAD FAT PROTEIN OPTIONAL CALORIES	CALORIES	CALORIES	CALORIES	CALORIES	CALORIES	CALORIES	CALORIES

WEEKLY CHECKLIST OF LIMITED PROTEIN EXCHANGES

EGGS ○ ○ ○

SEMISOFT OR HARD CHEESE ○ ○ ○

MEAT GROUP ○ ○ ○ ○ ○ ○ ○ ○ ○

LIVER ○ ○ ○

COMMENTS:

OCTOBER
NOVEMBER

1 9 8 5

MONDAY
28

TUESDAY
29

WEDNESDAY
30

Halloween

THURSDAY
31

FRIDAY
1

SATURDAY
2

SUNDAY
3

	S	M	T	W	T	F	S
SEPT	1	2	3	4	5	6	7
	8	9	10	11	12	13	14
	15	16	17	18	19	20	21
	22	23	24	25	26	27	28
	29	30					

	S	M	T	W	T	F	S
OCT			1	2	3	4	5
	6	7	8	9	10	11	12
	13	14	15	16	17	18	19
	20	21	22	23	24	25	26
	27	28	29	30	31		

	S	M	T	W	T	F	S
NOV						1	2
	3	4	5	6	7	8	9
	10	11	12	13	14	15	16
	17	18	19	20	21	22	23
	24	25	26	27	28	29	30

Cornish Hen in Pear Sauce

Long-Grain and Wild Rice with
Steamed Mushrooms

Cooked Diced Carrots

Iceberg Lettuce Wedge with
Reduced-Calorie Russian Dressing

Reduced-Calorie Vanilla Pudding

Coffee or Tea

HELPFUL HINTS: *Pear Sauce* is good on leftover poultry like chicken or turkey. Be sure to select firm, slightly underripe pears for cooking.

Tips for leftover rice: Enough to reheat? (1) Place in a large strainer in a saucepan of simmering water; cover and steam for 5 to 10 minutes; or (2) spread on a cookie sheet, sprinkle with a few drops of water, and bake at 350° F. for about 10 minutes. Just a little left? Add to chicken broth for a chicken-rice soup.

A WORD FROM JEAN NIDETCH: Don't let boredom ring the dinner bell. There's no reason to eat the same old meals over and over again. Be adventurous. Investigate new kinds of fruits, vegetables, fish, and meats to discover ones you haven't tasted before. Even familiar foods can be given an *un*familiar look—and taste—when they are prepared in new ways or simply seasoned differently. You may find you can create new family favorites.

PLAN FOR SUCCESS

What I succeeded at this week _____

_____

Goal for next week _____

Cornish Hen in Pear Sauce

Makes 2 servings

Hen

1¼-pound Cornish hen*
Dash each salt, pepper, and paprika
½ cup diced onion

Sauce

2 small pears, cored, pared, and cut into pieces
2 tablespoons each lemon juice and water
1 teaspoon each firmly packed brown sugar and
    thawed frozen concentrated pineapple
    juice (no sugar added)
Dash each ground ginger and ground cloves
1 tablespoon unsalted margarine, cut into pieces

To Prepare Hen: Preheat oven to 400°F. Place hen on rack in roasting pan. Lift skin and sprinkle meat with seasonings; stuff onions under skin and roast until hen is tender, about 40 minutes.

To Prepare Sauce: In blender container combine all ingredients except margarine and process until smooth. Transfer mixture to small saucepan; add margarine and cook over low heat, stirring constantly, until margarine is melted and mixture is heated.

To Serve: Remove skin and onions from hen and discard. Split hen in half and serve each portion with half of the sauce.

*A 1¼-pound Cornish hen will yield about 8 ounces cooked meat.

Each serving provides: 4 Protein Exchanges; 1½ Fat Exchanges; 1 Fruit Exchange; 15 calories Optional Exchange
Per serving: 391 calories, 34 g protein, 15 g fat, 32 g carbohydrate, 171 mg sodium, 101 mg cholesterol

WEEKLY FOOD DIARY

	MONDAY	TUESDAY	WEDNESDAY	THURSDAY	FRIDAY	SATURDAY	SUNDAY
BREAKFAST FRUIT PROTEIN BREAD FAT MILK OPTIONAL							
LUNCH PROTEIN BREAD VEGETABLES FAT FRUIT MILK OPTIONAL							
DINNER PROTEIN BREAD VEGETABLES FAT FRUIT MILK OPTIONAL							
SNACKS							
DAILY CHECK LIST FRUIT VEG. MILK BREAD FAT PROTEIN OPTIONAL	○○○○ ○○○○ ○○○○ ○○○○ ○○○○ ○○○○ □ CALORIES	○○○○ ○○○○ ○○○○ ○○○○ ○○○○ ○○○○ □ CALORIES	○○○○ ○○○○ ○○○○ ○○○○ ○○○○ ○○○○ □ CALORIES	○○○○ ○○○○ ○○○○ ○○○○ ○○○○ ○○○○ □ CALORIES	○○○○ ○○○○ ○○○○ ○○○○ ○○○○ ○○○○ □ CALORIES	○○○○ ○○○○ ○○○○ ○○○○ ○○○○ ○○○○ □ CALORIES	○○○○ ○○○○ ○○○○ ○○○○ ○○○○ ○○○○ □ CALORIES

WEEKLY CHECKLIST OF LIMITED PROTEIN EXCHANGES

EGGS ○○○○

SEMISOFT OR HARD CHEESE ○○○

MEAT GROUP ○○○○○○○○○○

LIVER ○○○

COMMENTS:

ENGAGEMENTS

NOVEMBER

1 9 8 5

MONDAY

4

Election Day

TUESDAY

5

WEDNESDAY

6

THURSDAY

7

FRIDAY

8

SATURDAY

9

SUNDAY

10

	S	M	T	W	T	F	S
			1	2	3	4	5
O	6	7	8	9	10	11	12
C	13	14	15	16	17	18	19
T	20	21	22	23	24	25	26
	27	28	29	30	31		

	S	M	T	W	T	F	S
						1	2
N	3	4	5	6	7	8	9
O	10	11	12	13	14	15	16
V	17	18	19	20	21	22	23
	24	25	26	27	28	29	30

	S	M	T	W	T	F	S
	1	2	3	4	5	6	7
D	8	9	10	11	12	13	14
E	15	16	17	18	19	20	21
C	22	23	24	25	26	27	28
	29	30	31				

Sherried Mushroom Soup

Baked Pork Chop

Boiled New Potatoes

Chilled Beet Salad

Sautéed Apple Slices and Raisins
with Instant Whipped Cream

Reduced-Calorie Hot Cocoa

HELPFUL HINTS: *To prepare mushrooms*, rinse gently in cool water, then shake lightly and blot dry (do not peel). To retain flavor and texture, cook for only 4 to 5 minutes.

Cooking tips for potatoes: To preserve nutritive value, boil with skins on in a minimum amount of water. To test for doneness, use a cake tester (a fork leaves too many holes, making potatoes watery). Pour off water and return saucepan to heat until sizzle stops. Skins will slip off easily.

A WORD FROM JEAN NIDETCH: Are you riding the mood-eating merry-go-round: eating because you're upset, then becoming more upset because you've gone on a binge? Next time you start to wander down the kitchen trail, take a short detour and head for some activity you can lose yourself in without gaining! And while you're at it, ask yourself whether you're really hungry for food—or for something else? The answer should keep you pointed in the right direction—away from the kitchen.

PLAN FOR SUCCESS

What I succeeded at this week _____

_____

Goal for next week _____

Sherried Mushroom Soup

Makes 2 servings

1 teaspoon margarine
½ cup diced onion
1 tablespoon plus 1 teaspoon
    all-purpose flour
2 cups sliced mushrooms
2 cups water
1 packet instant chicken broth
    and seasoning mix
⅛ teaspoon ground thyme
2 teaspoons dry sherry
Dash each salt and pepper
2 teaspoons chopped fresh parsley

In 1½- or 2-quart saucepan heat margarine until bubbly and hot; add onion and sauté, stirring occasionally, until softened, about 5 minutes. Add flour and cook, stirring constantly, until onion is lightly browned; add mushrooms and cook for 5 minutes longer. Stir in water, broth mix, and thyme and bring to a boil. Reduce heat and let simmer until slightly thickened, about 10 minutes; stir in sherry, salt, and pepper. Divide into 2 soup bowls and sprinkle each portion with 1 teaspoon parsley.

Each serving provides: 2½ Vegetable Exchanges; ½ Fat Exchange; 30 calories Optional Exchange
Per serving: 85 calories, 4 g protein, 2 g fat, 12 g carbohydrate, 519 mg sodium, 0 mg cholesterol

WEEKLY FOOD DIARY

	MONDAY	TUESDAY	WEDNESDAY	THURSDAY	FRIDAY	SATURDAY	SUNDAY
BREAKFAST FRUIT PROTEIN BREAD FAT MILK OPTIONAL							
LUNCH PROTEIN BREAD VEGETABLES FAT FRUIT MILK OPTIONAL							
DINNER PROTEIN BREAD VEGETABLES FAT FRUIT MILK OPTIONAL							
SNACKS							
DAILY CHECK LIST FRUIT VEG. MILK BREAD FAT PROTEIN OPTIONAL	○○○ ○○○ ○○○ ○○○ ○○○ ○○○○○○○ ☐ CALORIES	○○○ ○○○ ○○○ ○○○ ○○○ ○○○○○○○ ☐ CALORIES	○○○ ○○○ ○○○ ○○○ ○○○ ○○○○○○○ ☐ CALORIES	○○○ ○○○ ○○○ ○○○ ○○○ ○○○○○○○ ☐ CALORIES	○○○ ○○○ ○○○ ○○○ ○○○ ○○○○○○○ ☐ CALORIES	○○○ ○○○ ○○○ ○○○ ○○○ ○○○○○○○ ☐ CALORIES	○○○ ○○○ ○○○ ○○○ ○○○ ○○○○○○○ ☐ CALORIES

WEEKLY CHECKLIST OF LIMITED PROTEIN EXCHANGES

EGGS ○○○○

SEMISOFT OR HARD CHEESE ○○○

MEAT GROUP ○○○○○○○○○○

LIVER ○○○○○○

COMMENTS:

NOVEMBER

1 9 8 5

Veterans Day
Armistice Day (Canada)

MONDAY
11

TUESDAY
12

WEDNESDAY
13

THURSDAY
14

FRIDAY
15

SATURDAY
16

SUNDAY
17

OCT	S	M	T	W	T	F	S
			1	2	3	4	5
	6	7	8	9	10	11	12
	13	14	15	16	17	18	19
	20	21	22	23	24	25	26
	27	28	29	30	31		

NOV	S	M	T	W	T	F	S
						1	2
	3	4	5	6	7	8	9
	10	11	12	13	14	15	16
	17	18	19	20	21	22	23
	24	25	26	27	28	29	30

DEC	S	M	T	W	T	F	S
	1	2	3	4	5	6	7
	8	9	10	11	12	13	14
	15	16	17	18	19	20	21
	22	23	24	25	26	27	28
	29	30	31				

Roast Beef

Mashed Potatoes

Stir-Fried Broccoli Florets
and Yellow Squash

Glazed Onions

Baked Apple

Red Wine

HELPFUL HINTS: *To vary this week's recipe,* substitute sliced carrots for the onions; or make a colorful combination of both. This is one dish that should be prepared close to serving time for best results.

To touch up vegetables, try adding chopped celery or green pepper, seasoned bread crumbs, snipped chives, chopped pimiento, sliced stuffed olives, or shredded carrots.

A WORD FROM JEAN NIDETCH: It isn't realistic to expect family and friends to be mind readers. If you want their support and encouragement you should spell out precisely what you need. For example, tell them that when you perform well, some form of applause would give you a boost, but that when you make a mistake, the most helpful thing they can say or do is *nothing*. When a social hurdle is on the horizon, suggest specific ways you can be helped. Get into the habit of voicing your needs. Letting the words *out* may prevent food from going *in.*

PLAN FOR SUCCESS

What I succeeded at this week _____

_____

Goal for next week _____

Glazed Onions

Makes 4 servings

This is an excellent accompaniment to next week's roast turkey.

1 tablespoon plus 1 teaspoon
margarine
4 cups pearl onions
¼ teaspoon salt
1 tablespoon plus 1 teaspoon
firmly packed brown sugar
2 tablespoons water

In 12-inch skillet heat margarine until bubbly and hot; add onions and salt and sauté over low heat, stirring occasionally, until onions are thoroughly cooked, 20 to 25 minutes (to prevent onions from splitting or burning during cooking, stir gently with a wooden spoon). Sprinkle sugar over onions and continue sautéing until sugar melts; add water. Increase heat and bring to a boil, stirring gently and cooking until sugar mixture reduces and glazes onions; serve immediately.

Each serving provides: 2 Vegetable Exchanges; 1 Fat Exchange; 20 calories Optional Exchange
Per serving: 100 calories, 1 g protein, 4 g fat, 17 g carbohydrate, 192 mg sodium, 0 mg cholesterol

WEEKLY FOOD DIARY

DAILY CHECK LIST		MONDAY	TUESDAY	WEDNESDAY	THURSDAY	FRIDAY	SATURDAY	SUNDAY
BREAKFAST	FRUIT							
	PROTEIN							
	BREAD							
	FAT							
	MILK							
	OPTIONAL							
LUNCH	PROTEIN							
	BREAD							
	VEGETABLES							
	FAT							
	FRUIT							
	MILK							
	OPTIONAL							
DINNER	PROTEIN							
	BREAD							
	VEGETABLES							
	FAT							
	FRUIT							
	MILK							
	OPTIONAL							
SNACKS								
	FRUIT VEG. MILK BREAD FAT PROTEIN OPTIONAL	CALORIES	CALORIES	CALORIES	CALORIES	CALORIES	CALORIES	CALORIES

WEEKLY CHECKLIST OF LIMITED PROTEIN EXCHANGES

EGGS ○○○○

MEAT GROUP ○○○○○○○○○○○

SEMISOFT OR HARD CHEESE ○○○○

LIVER ○○○○

COMMENTS:

MONDAY
18

TUESDAY
19

WEDNESDAY
20

THURSDAY
21

FRIDAY
22

SATURDAY
23

SUNDAY
24

O C T	S	M	T	W	T	F	S
			1	2	3	4	5
	6	7	8	9	10	11	12
	13	14	15	16	17	18	19
	20	21	22	23	24	25	26
	27	28	29	30	31		

N O V	S	M	T	W	T	F	S
						1	2
	3	4	5	6	7	8	9
	10	11	12	13	14	15	16
	17	18	19	20	21	22	23
	24	25	26	27	28	29	30

D E C	S	M	T	W	T	F	S
	1	2	3	4	5	6	7
	8	9	10	11	12	13	14
	15	16	17	18	19	20	21
	22	23	24	25	26	27	28
	29	30	31				

Consommé

Roast Turkey

Honeyed Sweet Potatoes

Steamed Vegetable Medley

Tossed Salad with Herb Vinaigrette

Pumpkin Pudding Pie

Hot Apple Cider with Cinnamon Stick

HELPFUL HINTS: *Instead of making a pie,* just pour the pumpkin pudding filling into 8 individual parfait glasses. Sprinkle with unbaked graham cracker mixture.

Cooking tip: Using fresh pumpkin? A 5-pound pumpkin yields about 4½ cups mashed, cooked pumpkin. Use pumpkin to make bread, muffins, or custards.

Like to plan ahead? Save turkey leftovers to use in next week's recipe. Or make turkey tacos, turkey stew, and turkey croquettes. Turkey salad-in-a-pita makes a good office or school lunch.

A WORD FROM JEAN NIDETCH: The good word is that it is possible for you to celebrate Thanksgiving without stuffing *yourself.* If you're in charge of the feast, prepare "safe" adaptations of the traditional holiday dishes so you can join in, too. Do as much advance preparation as possible to avoid feeling like a "pressure cooker" (and pressure *eater*). And whether you are host or guest, keep encouraging yourself with positive messages so you can thank yourself when you get on the scale *after* Thanksgiving!

PLAN FOR SUCCESS

What I succeeded at this week _____

_____

Goal for next week _____

Pumpkin Pudding Pie

Makes 8 servings

Crust

10 graham crackers (2½-inch squares), made
    into crumbs
2 tablespoons plus 2 teaspoons margarine, softened

Filling

1 envelope (four ½-cup servings) reduced-calorie
    vanilla pudding mix
2 envelopes unflavored gelatin
1 tablespoon plus 1 teaspoon granulated sugar
2 cups skim milk
2 cups canned pumpkin
⅛ teaspoon ground cloves
Dash each ground nutmeg and ground ginger

To Prepare Crust: Preheat oven to 350°F. In bowl combine crumbs and margarine, mixing thoroughly. Using the back of a spoon, press crumb mixture over bottom and up sides of 9-inch pie pan. Bake until crisp and brown, about 15 minutes. Remove pan to a wire rack and let crust cool completely before filling.

To Prepare Filling: In 1-quart saucepan combine pudding mix, gelatin, and sugar; add milk and stir to combine. Let stand for about 1 minute to soften gelatin. Cook over medium heat until mixture comes to a boil.

In mixing bowl combine pumpkin and spices; using electric mixer, beat until combined. Add cooked pudding mixture and beat at low speed until thoroughly blended. Pour filling into cooled pie crust; cover and refrigerate until firm.

Each serving provides: ½ Bread Exchange; ½ Vegetable Exchange; 1 Fat Exchange; ½ Milk Exchange; 20 calories Optional Exchange

Per serving: 146 calories, 5 g protein, 5 g fat, 22 g carbohydrate, 284 mg sodium, 1 mg cholesterol

WEEKLY FOOD DIARY

	MONDAY	TUESDAY	WEDNESDAY	THURSDAY	FRIDAY	SATURDAY	SUNDAY
BREAKFAST FRUIT PROTEIN BREAD FAT MILK OPTIONAL							
LUNCH PROTEIN BREAD VEGETABLES FAT FRUIT MILK OPTIONAL							
DINNER PROTEIN BREAD VEGETABLES FAT FRUIT MILK OPTIONAL							
SNACKS							

DAILY CHECK LIST

FRUIT
VEG.
MILK
BREAD
FAT
PROTEIN
OPTIONAL

○○○○ ○○○○○ CALORIES ☐ (Monday through Sunday)

WEEKLY CHECKLIST OF LIMITED PROTEIN EXCHANGES

EGGS ○○○○

MEAT GROUP ○○○○○○○○

SEMISOFT OR HARD CHEESE ○○○○

LIVER ○○○○

COMMENTS:

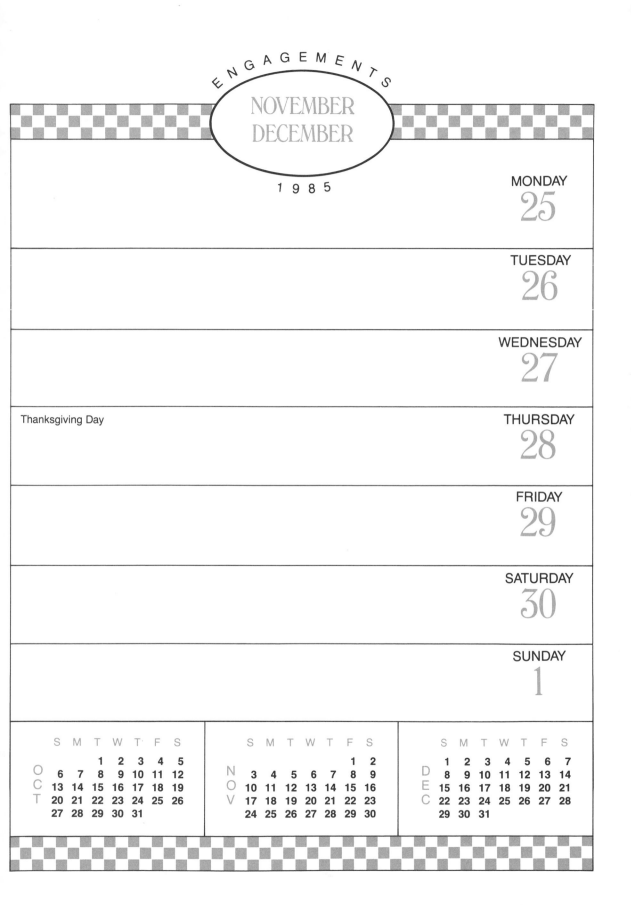

ENGAGEMENTS

NOVEMBER
DECEMBER

1 9 8 5

MONDAY
25

TUESDAY
26

WEDNESDAY
27

Thanksgiving Day

THURSDAY
28

FRIDAY
29

SATURDAY
30

SUNDAY
1

	S	M	T	W	T	F	S
OCT			1	2	3	4	5
	6	7	8	9	10	11	12
	13	14	15	16	17	18	19
	20	21	22	23	24	25	26
	27	28	29	30	31		

	S	M	T	W	T	F	S
NOV						1	2
	3	4	5	6	7	8	9
	10	11	12	13	14	15	16
	17	18	19	20	21	22	23
	24	25	26	27	28	29	30

	S	M	T	W	T	F	S
DEC	1	2	3	4	5	6	7
	8	9	10	11	12	13	14
	15	16	17	18	19	20	21
	22	23	24	25	26	27	28
	29	30	31				

Tomato Juice with Lime Wedge

Turkey Hash

Green Pepper and Cabbage Slaw
with Caraway Seed

Low-Calorie Gelatin with
Whipped Topping

Coffee or Tea

HELPFUL HINTS: *For a variation,* substitute chicken for the turkey, or try ground cooked ham instead.

Cooking tip: Potatoes may become slightly watery when they are shredded. To avoid spattering, remove the water before adding to the skillet.

Storage tip: Potatoes will keep in a cool, dry place (50° F.) for about 2 months. Never store them with onions; the moisture in potatoes will cause onions to sprout.

A WORD FROM JEAN NIDETCH: December launches a month of frantic holiday shopping, card-writing, and entertaining. It's easy to feel overwhelmed by everything that has to be done, and unfortunately that feeling can lead to overeating. There's one good prescription to head it off: sufficient doses of "Time for Me." Create an oasis of time just for yourself, preferably at an hour when you're most likely to feel down. Make it clear that you're unavailable as far as demands go during your break, and treat yourself to an activity you enjoy, like reading.

PLAN FOR SUCCESS

What I succeeded at this week _____

_____

Goal for next week _____

Turkey Hash

Makes 2 servings

The perfect recipe for using up leftover Thanksgiving turkey.

1 tablespoon vegetable oil
6 ounces peeled potatoes, shredded
½ cup each diced onion and green bell pepper
6 ounces skinned and boned cooked turkey, shredded
⅓ cup water
1 packet instant chicken broth and seasoning mix
Garnish: 1½ teaspoons chopped fresh parsley

In 10-inch nonstick skillet heat oil; add potatoes, onion, and pepper and sauté, stirring occasionally, until potatoes are cooked and browned. Stir in turkey, water, and broth mix and cook until mixture is heated and liquid is absorbed; serve sprinkled with parsley.

Each serving provides: 3 Protein Exchanges; 1 Bread Exchange; 1 Vegetable Exchange; 1½ Fat Exchanges; 5 calories Optional Exchange

Per serving: 299 calories, 28 g protein, 11 g fat, 21 g carbohydrate, 491 mg sodium, 65 mg cholesterol

Variation—Eggs 'n' Hash: Follow directions above; when liquid has been absorbed, using the back of a spoon, make 2 wells in hash. Slide 1 egg into each well; cover pan and cook until eggs are set.

Increase Protein Exchange to 4 Exchanges.

Per serving: 378 calories, 34 g protein, 17 g fat, 21 g carbohydrate, 560 mg sodium, 339 mg cholesterol

WEEKLY FOOD DIARY

	MONDAY	TUESDAY	WEDNESDAY	THURSDAY	FRIDAY	SATURDAY	SUNDAY
BREAKFAST FRUIT / PROTEIN / BREAD / FAT / MILK / OPTIONAL							
LUNCH PROTEIN / BREAD / VEGETABLES / FAT / FRUIT / MILK / OPTIONAL							
DINNER PROTEIN / BREAD / VEGETABLES / FAT / FRUIT / MILK / OPTIONAL							
SNACKS							
DAILY CHECK LIST FRUIT / VEG. / MILK / BREAD / FAT / PROTEIN / OPTIONAL	○○○ ○○○ ○○ ○○○ ○○ ○○○○ ○○○○○○ ☐ CALORIES	○○○ ○○○ ○○ ○○○ ○○ ○○○○ ○○○○○○ ☐ CALORIES	○○○ ○○○ ○○ ○○○ ○○ ○○○○ ○○○○○○ ☐ CALORIES	○○○ ○○○ ○○ ○○○ ○○ ○○○○ ○○○○○○ ☐ CALORIES	○○○ ○○○ ○○ ○○○ ○○ ○○○○ ○○○○○○ ☐ CALORIES	○○○ ○○○ ○○ ○○○ ○○ ○○○○ ○○○○○○ ☐ CALORIES	○○○ ○○○ ○○ ○○○ ○○ ○○○○ ○○○○○○ ☐ CALORIES

WEEKLY CHECKLIST OF LIMITED PROTEIN EXCHANGES

EGGS ○○○○

SEMISOFT OR HARD CHEESE ○○○○

MEAT GROUP ○○○○○○○○○○○○○○○

LIVER ○○○○○○

COMMENTS:

MONDAY
2

TUESDAY
3

WEDNESDAY
4

THURSDAY
5

FRIDAY
6

SATURDAY
7

Hanukkah

SUNDAY
8

	S	M	T	W	T	F	S
N						1	2
O	3	4	5	6	7	8	9
V	10	11	12	13	14	15	16
	17	18	19	20	21	22	23
	24	25	26	27	28	29	30

	S	M	T	W	T	F	S
D	1	2	3	4	5	6	7
E	8	9	10	11	12	13	14
C	15	16	17	18	19	20	21
	22	23	24	25	26	27	28
	29	30	31				

	S	M	T	W	T	F	S
J				1	2	3	4
A	5	6	7	8	9	10	11
N	12	13	14	15	16	17	18
	19	20	21	22	23	24	25
	26	27	28	29	30	31	

Roast Chicken

Quick Skillet Potato Pancakes

Steamed Green Beans and Cauliflower Florets

Sliced Cucumber and Tomato Wedges
on Lettuce with Oil and Vinegar Dressing

Pineapple Chunks

Tea with Lemon and Mint

HELPFUL HINTS: *For another taste,* serve Quick Skillet Potato Pancakes with a mixture of plain low-fat yogurt and chopped chives instead of applesauce. (Adjust Exchange Information accordingly.)

Keep cauliflower snowy white by adding a squirt of lemon juice as it cooks. Lemon juice keeps fresh fruit from discoloring too.

Time-saving tip: Make Potato Pancakes ahead and refrigerate; reheat in the oven prior to serving. Unfortunately, potato dishes generally do not freeze well; they tend to become mushy in texture.

A WORD FROM JEAN NIDETCH: Take a cue from champion athletes. They psych themselves before competitions by imagining each step. So instead of just hoping to survive a party, preview a mental film of your actions. SCENE: You walk in and head *away* from the buffet. SCENE: You hold a glass of wine or diet soda with *both* hands, so you can't take the hors d'oeuvres as they're passed around. SCENE: You use the same two-hands trick with a coffee cup, making the pastry tray impossible. . . . Award-winning performances all.

PLAN FOR SUCCESS

What I succeeded at this week _____

_____

Goal for next week _____

Quick Skillet Potato Pancakes

Makes 2 servings, 2 pancakes each

⅓ cup instant mashed potato flakes
3 tablespoons self-rising flour
½ cup skim milk
¼ cup minced onion
1 egg, beaten
⅛ teaspoon salt
Dash each pepper and ground nutmeg
1 tablespoon vegetable oil
½ cup applesauce (no sugar added)

In small bowl combine potato flakes and flour; add remaining ingredients except oil and applesauce and, using a fork, blend thoroughly.

In 10-inch nonstick skillet heat oil; drop batter into skillet by heaping tablespoonsful, forming 4 pancakes. Cook until bottoms of pancakes are browned; turn pancakes and brown other side. Remove to serving plate and serve with applesauce.

Each serving provides: ½ Protein Exchange; 1 Bread Exchange; ¼ Vegetable Exchange; 1½ Fat Exchanges; ½ Fruit Exchange; ¼ Milk Exchange
Per serving: 230 calories, 7 g protein, 10 g fat, 28 g carbohydrate, 347 mg sodium, 138 mg cholesterol

WEEKLY FOOD DIARY

	MONDAY	TUESDAY	WEDNESDAY	THURSDAY	FRIDAY	SATURDAY	SUNDAY
BREAKFAST FRUIT PROTEIN BREAD FAT MILK OPTIONAL							
LUNCH PROTEIN BREAD VEGETABLES FAT FRUIT MILK OPTIONAL							
DINNER PROTEIN BREAD VEGETABLES FAT FRUIT MILK OPTIONAL							
SNACKS							
DAILY CHECK LIST FRUIT VEG. MILK BREAD FAT PROTEIN OPTIONAL	○○○ ○○○ ○○○ ○○○ ○○○ ○○○○○○ CALORIES	○○○ ○○○ ○○○ ○○○ ○○○ ○○○○○○ CALORIES	○○○ ○○○ ○○○ ○○○ ○○○ ○○○○○○ CALORIES	○○○ ○○○ ○○○ ○○○ ○○○ ○○○○○○ CALORIES	○○○ ○○○ ○○○ ○○○ ○○○ ○○○○○○ CALORIES	○○○ ○○○ ○○○ ○○○ ○○○ ○○○○○○ CALORIES	○○○ ○○○ ○○○ ○○○ ○○○ ○○○○○○ CALORIES

WEEKLY CHECKLIST OF LIMITED PROTEIN EXCHANGES

EGGS ○○○ ○○○

MEAT GROUP ○○○○○○○○○

LIVER ○○○○○○

SEMISOFT OR HARD CHEESE ○○○ ○○○

COMMENTS:

ENGAGEMENTS

DECEMBER

1985

MONDAY
9

TUESDAY
10

WEDNESDAY
11

THURSDAY
12

FRIDAY
13

SATURDAY
14

SUNDAY
15

	S	M	T	W	T	F	S
						1	2
NOV	3	4	5	6	7	8	9
	10	11	12	13	14	15	16
	17	18	19	20	21	22	23
	24	25	26	27	28	29	30

	S	M	T	W	T	F	S
	1	2	3	4	5	6	7
DEC	8	9	10	11	12	13	14
	15	16	17	18	19	20	21
	22	23	24	25	26	27	28
	29	30	31				

	S	M	T	W	T	F	S
				1	2	3	4
JAN	5	6	7	8	9	10	11
	12	13	14	15	16	17	18
	19	20	21	22	23	24	25
	26	27	28	29	30	31	

French Ham 'n' Cheese Sandwich

Pickle Slices

Cauliflower Florets and Carrot Sticks

Fruit Cocktail

Beer

HELPFUL HINTS: *Vary this week's recipe* by substituting rye bread for whole wheat, skinned sliced cooked turkey or chicken for ham, Muenster cheese for Swiss, and for a "hotter" sandwich, use Dijon-style mustard.

For school or office lunch, prepare sandwiches (omitting tomato slices) but do not dip in beaten egg. Place in freezer bags, label and freeze. Frozen sandwiches can be kept for 2 weeks. Just be sure not to use ingredients like lettuce, celery, cucumber, jelly, mayonnaise, or tomatoes. (Adjust Protein Exchange Information to 2 Exchanges.)

A WORD FROM JEAN NIDETCH: Mentally code foods in traffic-light style: STOP, GO, and CAUTION. STOPS are foods that could *stop* your progress: best to banish them or insist they be kept out of sight. GOS are items you can handle in ways that keep you headed in the right direction. CAUTION means foods that can usually be eaten, but may become hazardous when stress strikes. *Plan ahead.* If a stressful time is on the horizon, get CAUTION foods out of your path.

PLAN FOR SUCCESS

What I succeeded at this week _____

_____

Goal for next week _____

French Ham 'n' Cheese Sandwich

Makes 2 servings

2 eggs
4 slices whole wheat bread
1 tablespoon plus 1 teaspoon margarine, divided
2 teaspoons prepared mustard
2 ounces each sliced boiled ham and Swiss cheese
1 medium tomato, thinly sliced

In shallow bowl beat eggs; set aside.

Spread 2 bread slices with 1 teaspoon margarine each; spread remaining 2 slices with 1 teaspoon mustard each. Top each mustard-spread slice with 1 ounce ham, 1 ounce cheese, and half of the tomato slices, then 1 bread slice, margarine-side down.

Dip each sandwich into beaten eggs, turning once and allowing both sides to absorb as much egg as possible.

In 12-inch nonstick skillet heat remaining 2 teaspoons margarine until bubbly and hot; add sandwiches and pour any remaining egg over bread. Cook over medium-high heat, turning once, until browned on both sides. Reduce heat, cover, and cook until cheese is melted, about 5 minutes. To serve, cut each sandwich into quarters.

Each serving provides: 3 Protein Exchanges; 2 Bread Exchanges; 1 Vegetable Exchange; 2 Fat Exchanges
Per serving: 437 calories, 27 g protein, 25 g fat, 27 g carbohydrate, 798 mg sodium, 326 mg cholesterol

WEEKLY FOOD DIARY

	MONDAY	TUESDAY	WEDNESDAY	THURSDAY	FRIDAY	SATURDAY	SUNDAY
BREAKFAST FRUIT PROTEIN BREAD FAT MILK OPTIONAL							
LUNCH PROTEIN BREAD VEGETABLES FAT FRUIT MILK OPTIONAL							
DINNER PROTEIN BREAD VEGETABLES FAT FRUIT MILK OPTIONAL							
SNACKS							
DAILY CHECK LIST FRUIT VEG. MILK BREAD FAT PROTEIN OPTIONAL CALORIES	○○○○○○○○ ○○○○ ○○○○ ○○○○○○○○ ○○○○○○○○ ○○○○ ☐ CALORIES	○○○○○○○○ ○○○○ ○○○○ ○○○○○○○○ ○○○○○○○○ ○○○○ ☐ CALORIES	○○○○○○○○ ○○○○ ○○○○ ○○○○○○○○ ○○○○○○○○ ○○○○ ☐ CALORIES	○○○○○○○○ ○○○○ ○○○○ ○○○○○○○○ ○○○○○○○○ ○○○○ ☐ CALORIES	○○○○○○○○ ○○○○ ○○○○ ○○○○○○○○ ○○○○○○○○ ○○○○ ☐ CALORIES	○○○○○○○○ ○○○○ ○○○○ ○○○○○○○○ ○○○○○○○○ ○○○○ ☐ CALORIES	○○○○○○○○ ○○○○ ○○○○ ○○○○○○○○ ○○○○○○○○ ○○○○ ☐ CALORIES

WEEKLY CHECKLIST OF LIMITED PROTEIN EXCHANGES

EGGS ○○○○	MEAT GROUP ○○○○○○○○	
SEMISOFT OR HARD CHEESE ○○○○	LIVER ○○○○	

COMMENTS:

MONDAY
16

TUESDAY
17

WEDNESDAY
18

THURSDAY
19

FRIDAY
20

SATURDAY
21

SUNDAY
22

	S	M	T	W	T	F	S
						1	2
N	3	4	5	6	7	8	9
O	10	11	12	13	14	15	16
V	17	18	19	20	21	22	23
	24	25	26	27	28	29	30

	S	M	T	W	T	F	S
	1	2	3	4	5	6	7
D	8	9	10	11	12	13	14
E	15	16	17	18	19	20	21
C	22	23	24	25	26	27	28
	29	30	31				

	S	M	T	W	T	F	S
				1	2	3	4
J	5	6	7	8	9	10	11
A	12	13	14	15	16	17	18
N	19	20	21	22	23	24	25
	26	27	28	29	30	31	

Roast Loin of Pork

Baked Acorn Squash Rings

Steamed Broccoli Spears with
Sesame Seed

Celery and Olive Tray

Fig Pastries

Red Wine

HELPFUL HINTS: *To save time,* bake Fig Pastries a day ahead and warm them in the oven. Or prepare and fill dough early in the day and refrigerate covered with foil on a baking sheet to be baked right before serving.

Storage tips: To maintain moistness, store boxed dried fruit in a plastic bag in refrigerator. Store leftover raisins in a covered glass jar in refrigerator with several pieces of lemon or orange peel. Raisins stay moist indefinitely and take on a nice flavor.

A WORD FROM JEAN NIDETCH: A dangerous feature of the Christmas season is the annual office party. Jockey for the best spot—away from the food, and when you do eat, be selective. If you've saved your allotment of wine for this event, remember that it goes further when it's paired with club soda. Or opt for liquor-less diet soda, salt-free seltzer, or tomato juice. The bonus for all this is that you'll find yourself in line for promotion to a better shape.

PLAN FOR SUCCESS

What I succeeded at this week _____

_____

Goal for next week _____

Fig Pastries

Makes 4 servings

⅓ cup plus 2 teaspoons all-purpose flour
1 tablespoon plus 1 teaspoon margarine
2 to 3 tablespoons ice water
3 large dried figs, plumped in hot water,
    drained, and chopped
2 tablespoons raisins, chopped
2 teaspoons firmly packed brown sugar
1 teaspoon grated orange peel
Dash each ground cinnamon, ground nutmeg,
    and ground mace

In small bowl, with pastry blender or 2 knives used scissors-fashion, combine flour and margarine, cutting in margarine until mixture resembles coarse meal; add ice water and mix until thoroughly combined (dough should just hold together but should not be sticky). Form dough into 4 equal balls; wrap each in plastic wrap and refrigerate for at least 1 hour.

In small bowl combine remaining ingredients. Roll each ball of dough between 2 sheets of wax paper, forming four 5-inch circles; spoon ¼ of fruit mixture onto center of each and, using fingers, spread filling in narrow line along diameter of circle. Roll each to enclose filling, pressing edges to seal; using small knife, cut 4 slits in top of each pastry. Transfer pastries to nonstick baking sheet and bake at 400°F. until golden brown, about 20 minutes.

Each serving provides: ½ Bread Exchange; 1 Fat Exchange; 1 Fruit Exchange; 10 calories Optional Exchange

Per serving: 139 calories, 2 g protein, 4 g fat, 25 g carbohydrate, 48 mg sodium, 0 mg cholesterol

WEEKLY FOOD DIARY

	MONDAY	TUESDAY	WEDNESDAY	THURSDAY	FRIDAY	SATURDAY	SUNDAY
BREAKFAST FRUIT PROTEIN BREAD FAT MILK OPTIONAL							
LUNCH PROTEIN BREAD VEGETABLES FAT FRUIT MILK OPTIONAL							
DINNER PROTEIN BREAD VEGETABLES FAT FRUIT MILK OPTIONAL							
SNACKS							
DAILY CHECK LIST FRUIT VEG. MILK BREAD FAT PROTEIN OPTIONAL	○○○○○○○ ○○○○○○○ □ CALORIES	○○○○○○○ ○○○○○○○ □ CALORIES	○○○○○○○ ○○○○○○○ □ CALORIES	○○○○○○○ ○○○○○○○ □ CALORIES	○○○○○○○ ○○○○○○○ □ CALORIES	○○○○○○○ ○○○○○○○ □ CALORIES	○○○○○○○ ○○○○○○○ □ CALORIES

WEEKLY CHECKLIST OF LIMITED PROTEIN EXCHANGES

EGGS ○○○○

SEMISOFT OR ○○○
HARD CHEESE

MEAT GROUP ○○○○○○○○○○○

LIVER ○○○○

COMMENTS:

MONDAY
23

TUESDAY
24

Christmas

WEDNESDAY
25

Boxing Day (Canada)

THURSDAY
26

FRIDAY
27

SATURDAY
28

SUNDAY
29

	S	M	T	W	T	F	S
N						1	2
O	3	4	5	6	7	8	9
V	10	11	12	13	14	15	16
	17	18	19	20	21	22	23
	24	25	26	27	28	29	30

	S	M	T	W	T	F	S
	1	2	3	4	5	6	7
D	8	9	10	11	12	13	14
E	15	16	17	18	19	20	21
C	22	23	24	25	26	27	28
	29	30	31				

	S	M	T	W	T	F	S
				1	2	3	4
J	5	6	7	8	9	10	11
A	12	13	14	15	16	17	18
N	19	20	21	22	23	24	25
	26	27	28	29	30	31	

Stuffed Mushrooms

Roast Beef

Baked Potato Topped with
Plain Low-Fat Yogurt and Chopped Chives

Steamed Brussels Sprouts with
Lemon Margarine

Vanilla Dietary Frozen Dessert
with Canned Peach Slices

Champagne

HELPFUL HINTS: *Adapt this week's recipe* for use as a snack or side dish as well as an appetizer. The stuffing can be varied; try fillings of cooked chopped spinach or carrots or seasoned cooked rice.

Some tips on mushrooms: Except when stuffing, always buy small mushrooms with soft stems; they are a better buy. Never soak or wash mushrooms until just before using.

A WORD FROM JEAN NIDETCH: The slang phrase "to eighty-six something" means to get rid of it. In 1986, how about "86-ing" that "you" who keeps saying, "I don't like myself," and who specializes in mental reruns of every mistake to justify that awful-me image? Instead, start rehearsing the words: "I like myself." Reinforce them by constantly reminding yourself of your *strong* points. List all the things you do well; the length of the list might astound you. That's the way to go from strength to strength, for succeeding begins with *believing* you can. Try that thought on for size in 1986!

PLAN FOR SUCCESS

What I succeeded at this week _____

_____

Goal for next week _____

Stuffed Mushrooms

Makes 4 servings

12 large mushrooms (2-inch diameter each)
1 tablespoon plus 1 teaspoon margarine
2 tablespoons minced onion
1 small garlic clove, minced
2 teaspoons dry white wine
⅓ cup plus 2 teaspoons plain dried bread crumbs
1 tablespoon plus 1 teaspoon grated Parmesan cheese
¼ teaspoon each salt and basil leaves
Dash pepper

Remove stems from mushrooms, reserving caps; finely chop stems. In small skillet heat margarine over medium heat until bubbly and hot; add chopped mushroom stems, onion, and garlic and sauté until tender. Add wine and cook for 1 minute; remove from heat and stir in remaining ingredients.

Preheat oven to 350°F. Spray a nonstick baking sheet with nonstick cooking spray. Stuff an equal amount of mushroom mixture into each mushroom cap and arrange caps on sprayed sheet; bake until mushrooms are cooked, 15 to 20 minutes.

Each serving provides: ½ Bread Exchange; 2 Vegetable Exchanges; 1 Fat Exchange; 15 calories Optional Exchange

Per serving: 111 calories, 5 g protein, 5 g fat, 12 g carbohydrate, 297 mg sodium, 2 mg cholesterol

WEEKLY FOOD DIARY

	MONDAY	TUESDAY	WEDNESDAY	THURSDAY	FRIDAY	SATURDAY	SUNDAY
BREAKFAST FRUIT PROTEIN BREAD FAT MILK OPTIONAL							
LUNCH PROTEIN BREAD VEGETABLES FAT FRUIT MILK OPTIONAL							
DINNER PROTEIN BREAD VEGETABLES FAT FRUIT MILK OPTIONAL							
SNACKS							
DAILY CHECK LIST FRUIT VEG. MILK BREAD FAT PROTEIN OPTIONAL	○○○ ○○○ ○○○○ ○○○○ ○○○○○○○ ◻ CALORIES	○○ ○○○ ○○○○ ○○○○○○○○ ◻ CALORIES	○○○ ○○○○ ○○○○ ○○○○○○○ ◻ CALORIES	○○○ ○○○ ○○○○ ○○○○○○○ ◻ CALORIES	○○○ ○○○ ○○○○ ○○○○○○○ ◻ CALORIES	○○○ ○○○ ○○○○ ○○○○○○○ ◻ CALORIES	○○○ ○○○ ○○○○ ○○○○○○○ ◻ CALORIES

WEEKLY CHECKLIST OF LIMITED PROTEIN EXCHANGES

EGGS ○○○ ○○○

MEAT GROUP ○○○○○○○○○○

LIVER ○○○○○○

SEMISOFT OR HARD CHEESE ○○○

COMMENTS:

ENGAGEMENTS

DECEMBER
JANUARY

1985

MONDAY
30

TUESDAY
31

New Year's Day 1986

WEDNESDAY
1

THURSDAY
2

FRIDAY
3

SATURDAY
4

SUNDAY
5

	S	M	T	W	T	F	S
						1	2
N	3	4	5	6	7	8	9
O	10	11	12	13	14	15	16
V	17	18	19	20	21	22	23
	24	25	26	27	28	29	30

	S	M	T	W	T	F	S
	1	2	3	4	5	6	7
D	8	9	10	11	12	13	14
E	15	16	17	18	19	20	21
C	22	23	24	25	26	27	28
	29	30	31				

	S	M	T	W	T	F	S
				1	2	3	4
J	5	6	7	8	9	10	11
A	12	13	14	15	16	17	18
N	19	20	21	22	23	24	25
	26	27	28	29	30	31	

Eating lunches out need not prevent anyone from staying on a weight-control program. It's easy to pack up or order out a delicious and nutritious meal and still stay within the guidelines of the Weight Watchers Full Exchange Plan. Here are some suggestions for easy and convenient lunches that can be packed in a bag or ordered at a restaurant. If any suggested item is seasonally unavailable or not to your liking, substitutions may be made by referring to the Food Plan for appropriate alternatives.

Take-Along Lunches

2 ounces Cheddar or Swiss cheese
6 sesame melba rounds
Tomato and cucumber slices
1 small pear

Salmon salad (2 ounces drained canned salmon with chopped celery
        and 2 teaspoons mayonnaise) on 2 thin slices (½ ounce each)
        whole wheat bread.
Carrot sticks
1 small apple

2 ounces liverwurst, 1 ounce American cheese, and lettuce leaves with
        mustard on 1 slice white bread
Cauliflower and broccoli florets
2 medium plums

Egg salad (2 hard-cooked eggs, chopped, with chopped onion and
        celery and 2 teaspoons mayonnaise) on 2-ounce pita bread
Cherry tomatoes
1 small nectarine

2 tablespoons peanut butter and 1 tablespoon reduced-calorie
        fruit-flavored spread on 1 slice raisin bread
Whole green beans and red bell pepper slices
1 small orange

2 ounces drained canned tuna and 1 hard-cooked egg, sliced, on
        1 toasted English muffin
Whole mushrooms and zucchini slices
10 large cherries

2 ounces sliced boiled ham and 1 ounce sliced Swiss cheese with
        1½ teaspoons Russian dressing on 2 slices pumpernickel
        bread
Green bell pepper slices
1 medium peach

3 ounces sliced skinned roast chicken with lettuce leaves and
    2 teaspoons ketchup on 2-ounce rye roll
Celery and carrot sticks
20 small or 12 large grapes

"Reuben Sandwich" (2 ounces sliced skinned roast turkey and
    1 ounce sliced Swiss cheese with drained sauerkraut on
    2 slices rye bread)
1 medium dill pickle
1 large tangerine

1 ounce each sliced provolone and prosciutto, rolled up, with
    lettuce and mustard on 2-ounce frankfurter roll
Zucchini and carrot sticks
¾ ounce dried apple slices

2 tablespoons peanut butter and ¼ medium banana, sliced, on
    2 graham crackers (2½-inch squares)
Carrot sticks
1 medium plum

Chicken-Cheddar salad (2 ounces skinned diced chicken, 1 ounce
    shredded Cheddar cheese, and 2 teaspoons mayonnaise) on
    2-ounce bagel
Lettuce leaves and red onion slices
2 medium apricots

Restaurant Lunches

2 to 4 ounces broiled hamburger
2-ounce hamburger roll
½ cup coleslaw
½ cup applesauce
Diet soda

Turkey sandwich (2 to 4 ounces skinned roast turkey on 2 slices
    bread)
Tossed salad with 1 tablespoon Italian dressing
¼ small cantaloupe
Iced tea

¼ roast chicken (3 to 4 ounces skinned and boned meat)
3 ounces baked potato with 1 teaspoon margarine
Sliced tomato on lettuce with 1 teaspoon mayonnaise
½ cup fruit salad
Coffee or tea

3- to 4-ounce broiled or baked fish fillet (no fat added) with
    lemon wedges
¾ ounce breadsticks or 1-ounce roll
Vegetable of the day (no fat added)
Sparkling mineral water

Individual can of tuna or salmon (about 3 ounces drained weight)
1-ounce roll with 1 teaspoon margarine
Sliced onion and tomato
½ medium grapefruit
Iced coffee or tea

Chef's salad (1 ounce each skinned roast turkey, boiled ham, and
    roast beef, and 1 hard-cooked egg, sliced, on tossed salad
    with 1 tablespoon French dressing)
1-ounce roll
Coffee or tea

Open-face grilled cheese and tomato sandwich (2 ounces American
    cheese and tomato slices on 1 or 2 slices bread)
Vegetable of the day (no fat added)
Tossed salad with 1 tablespoon blue cheese dressing
Diet soda

2-ounce frankfurter with mustard and 1 tablespoon ketchup on
    2-ounce frankfurter roll
½ cup hot sauerkraut
Iced tea with lemon

3 to 4 ounces broiled shrimp with lemon wedges (no fat added)
½ cup cooked rice (plain)
Vegetable of the day (no fat added)
½ cup fruit-flavored gelatin

Cottage cheese and fresh fruit platter (⅔ to 1 cup cottage cheese,
    ½ cup cut-up fresh fruit, and ½ cup fruit-flavored gelatin)
4 melba toast slices or 6 melba rounds
Tossed salad with 1 tablespoon Russian dressing
Iced coffee or tea

WEIGHT WATCHERS DIRECTORY
United States and Canada

ALABAMA
Northern state   305-964-8100
Southern state   305-841-4971

ALASKA
Anchorage   907-279-3232
Remainder of state 907-279-3232 (call Collect)

ARIZONA
Phoenix   602-248-0303
Tucson   602-881-0157

ARKANSAS
Eastern Arkansas   901-327-6114
Little Rock   501-227-6500

CALIFORNIA
Eastern Los Angeles County   213-571-6616
Fresno area   209-222-4458
Kern County   805-872-1506
L.A./San Fernando Valley   818-995-4371
Orange County   714-835-5505
San Diego County   714-286-0120
Sacramento area   916-483-4951
San Francisco/Bay area   415-864-8282
San Jose/Santa Clara County   408-379-3325
Ventura County   805-526-4528

COLORADO
Denver   303-795-6111

CONNECTICUT
Eastern state   203-877-7431
Milford   203-877-7431

DELAWARE
Entire state   804-425-8446

FLORIDA
Ft. Lauderdale/Broward County   305-525-7233
Ft. Myers area   813-936-0306
Jacksonville/northeastern Florida 904-721-2740
Miami/Dade County   305-221-9411
Orlando   305-841-4971
Tampa/Hillsborough County   813-877-6796
St. Petersburg/Pinellas County   813-461-1801
West Palm Beach   305-964-8100
Sarasota   813-953-6650

GEORGIA
Atlanta   404-373-5731
Southern state   904-721-2740

HAWAII
Entire state   808-955-1588

IDAHO
Northern state   509-327-4484
Southern state   801-486-0125
Boise   208-336-1180

ILLINOIS
Chicago/northern state   312-325-8700
Central state   217-793-1640
Southern state   314-878-1000

INDIANA
Southeastern state 513-851-8800 (call Collect)
Central Indiana   317-846-7546
Northern state   219-277-4050 (call Collect)
Southern state   502-426-7800
Northwestern state   312-325-8700

IOWA
Des Moines/western state   515-278-4357
Southeastern state   217-793-1640

KANSAS	
Greater Kansas City area	913-649-2070
Remainder of state	316-265-2641 (call Collect)

KENTUCKY	
Northern state	513-851-8800 (call Collect)
Boyd County	304-346-0609
Remainder of state	316-265-2641 (call Collect)

LOUISIANA	
Entire state	504-368-5400

MAINE	
Entire state	207-781-4403

MARYLAND	
Baltimore	301-484-0577
Central & southern state	301-770-4115
Eastern Shore	804-425-8446

MASSACHUSETTS	
Eastern state	617-566-5100
Springfield	413-786-6611
Worcester	617-753-9173

MICHIGAN	
Northern state	616-947-0010
Upper Peninsula	906-228-6123
Ann Arbor area	313-663-2365
Detroit area	313-557-5454
Northern state	616-947-0010
Tri-Cities & Thumb area	517-799-6650
Western & central state	517-394-1631
Flint area	313-623-9077 (call Collect)

MINNESOTA	
Entire state	612-546-3546

MISSISSIPPI	
Jackson	601-982-5783
Southern state	504-368-4500

MISSOURI	
Columbia area	314-696-3773
Kansas City/western state	913-649-2070
St. Louis	314-878-1000
Springfield	417-881-8688

MONTANA	
Entire state	509-327-4484

NEBRASKA	
Eastern state	402-333-4357
Western state	303-795-6111

NEVADA	
Reno	702-323-4459
Las Vegas	702-736-6683
Northeastern state	801-486-0127

NEW HAMPSHIRE	
Entire state	603-882-1261

NEW JERSEY	
Bergen & Hudson Counties	201-265-3900
North, central, & southern state	201-992-8600
W. Burlington, Camden, & Gloucester Counties	215-548-3600

NEW MEXICO	
Albuquerque area	505-266-5786
Santa Fe area	505-983-4222
Southeastern state	915-593-7208

NEW YORK	
Adirondack area	518-584-8466
Albany area	518-489-8323
Binghamton area	607-724-2404
Clinton County	802-658-1920
Nassau County	516-627-8905
New York City	212-896-9800
Rockland County	914-634-7809
Rochester area	716-232-7636
Suffolk County	516-587-4500
Syracuse area	315-455-5776
Utica/Herkimer areas	315-724-4618
Westchester County	914-423-1200
Western state	716-837-4141

NORTH CAROLINA	
Asheville area	704-274-0156
Central state	919-295-6896
Eastern Shore	804-425-8446
Raleigh/eastern state	919-876-1050

NORTH DAKOTA	
Eastern state	509-327-4484
Remainder of state	612-546-3546

OHIO

Central state	614-457-9080
Cincinnati	513-851-8800
Cleveland	216-921-7700
Lawrence County	304-346-0609
Steubenville area	412-521-9300
Lima area	419-227-5517
Toledo area	419-472-6003

OKLAHOMA

Oklahoma City/remainder of state	405-843-9611
North central state	316-265-2641

OREGON

Southwestern state	503-342-5386
Remainder of state	503-297-1021

PENNSYLVANIA

Allentown/Bethlehem/Easton	215-791-1141
Central state	717-763-1290
Northwestern state	814-868-4684
Pittsburgh	412-521-9300
Northeastern state/Scranton/ Wilkes-Barre	215-791-1141
Southeastern state	215-548-3600

RHODE ISLAND

Entire state	401-942-6900

SOUTH CAROLINA

Charleston area	803-571-5200
Columbia area	803-798-1050
Greenville area	803-242-9276

SOUTH DAKOTA

Eastern state	612-546-3546
Rapid City area	303-795-6111

TENNESSEE

Chattanooga/southern state	615-877-1181
Memphis/western state	901-327-6114
Northeastern state	304-346-0609
Central and eastern state	615-383-5900

TEXAS

Austin	512-454-5661
Corpus Christi	512-992-7771
San Antonio area	512-341-6247
Dallas	214-369-2341
Eastern state	214-561-4238
Far west state	915-593-7208
Ft. Worth	817-277-5531
Houston area	713-772-7715
Amarillo	806-355-9744
Lubbock	806-795-5571

UTAH

Southwestern area	702-736-6683
Remainder of state	801-486-0125

VERMONT

Bennington & Windham Counties	518-584-8466
Remainder of state	802-658-1920

VIRGINIA

Fairfax County	703-532-2960
Remainder of state	804-425-8446

WASHINGTON

Clark County	503-297-1021
Seattle	206-525-2323
Eastern state/Spokane	509-327-4484

WASHINGTON, D.C.

Entire D.C.	301-770-4115

WEST VIRGINIA

Charleston	304-346-0609
Wheeling	304-232-2817

WISCONSIN

Milwaukee area	414-963-1010
Western area	612-546-3546

WYOMING

Eastern state	303-795-6111
Western state	801-486-0125

CANADA

Montreal, Que.	514-482-9800
Quebec, Que.	418-651-9224
Trois Rivieres, Que.	819-378-3655
Hull, Que.	819-770-4108
Saskatchewan, Sask.	306-652-8446
Edmonton, Alta.	403-424-6491
Calgary, Alta.	403-252-7523
Vancouver, B.C.	604-524-4441
Victoria, B.C.	604-727-5121
Winnipeg, Man.	204-942-4284

Brandon, Man.	204-728-8797	Toronto, Ont.	416-826-9200
Kitchener, Ont.	519-886-8280	Windsor, Ont.	519-944-6000
London, Ont.	519-455-5100	Dartmouth, N.S.	902-463-7041
St. Caterines, Ont.	416-682-2603	St. John, N.B.	506-847-2508
Hamilton, Ont.	416-560-7386	Moncton, N.B.	506-854-3388
North Bay, Ont.	705-474-6725	Fredericton, N.B.	506-472-5642
Orilla, Ont.	705-726-5505	Nova Scotia	902-454-6400
Ottawa, Ont.	613-725-1200	Chatham, N.B.	506-773-7800
Sault Ste. Marie, Ont.	705-949-3500	St. John's, Nfd.	709-579-0139
Sudbury, Ont.	705-560-0333	Charlottetown, P.E.I.	902-675-3511

Dry and Liquid Measure Equivalents

Teaspoons	Tablespoons	Cups	Fluid Ounces
3 teaspoons	1 tablespoon		½ fluid ounce
6 teaspoons	2 tablespoons	⅛ cup	1 fluid ounce
12 teaspoons	4 tablespoons	¼ cup	2 fluid ounces
16 teaspoons	5 tablespoons plus 1 teaspoon	⅓ cup	
18 teaspoons	6 tablespoons	⅓ cup plus 2 teaspoons	3 fluid ounces
24 teaspoons	8 tablespoons	½ cup	4 fluid ounces
30 teaspoons	10 tablespoons	½ cup plus 2 tablespoons	5 fluid ounces
32 teaspoons	10 tablespoons plus 2 teaspoons	⅔ cup	
36 teaspoons	12 tablespoons	¾ cup	6 fluid ounces
42 teaspoons	14 tablespoons	1 cup less 2 tablespoons	7 fluid ounces
48 teaspoons	16 tablespoons	1 cup	8 fluid ounces
96 teaspoons	32 tablespoons	2 cups (1 pint)	16 fluid ounces
		4 cups (1 quart)	32 fluid ounces

Note: Measurements of less than ⅛ teaspoon are considered a dash or a pinch.

Weight Watchers Metric Conversion Table

WEIGHT

To Change	To	Multiply by
Ounces	Grams	30.0
Pounds	Kilograms	0.48

VOLUME

To Change	To	Multiply by
Teaspoons	Milliliters	5.0
Tablespoons	Milliliters	15.0
Cups	Milliliters	250.0
Cups	Liters	0.25
Pints	Liters	0.5
Quarts	Liters	1.0
Gallons	Liters	4.0

LENGTH

To Change	To	Multiply by
Inches	Millimeters	25.0
Inches	Centimeters	2.5
Feet	Centimeters	30.0
Yards	Meters	0.9

TEMPERATURE

To change degrees Fahrenheit to degrees Celsius subtract **32°** and multiply by ⁵⁄₉.

Oven Temperatures

Degrees Fahrenheit =	Degrees Celsius	Degrees Fahrenheit =	Degrees Celsius
250	120	400	200
275	140	425	220
300	150	450	230
325	160	475	250
350	180	500	260
375	190	525	270

METRIC SYMBOLS

Symbol =	Metric Unit	Symbol =	Metric Unit
g	gram	C°	degrees Celsius
kg	kilogram	mm	millimeter
ml	milliliter	cm	centimeter
l	liter	m	meter

1984

JANUARY
S	M	T	W	T	F	S
1	2	3	4	5	6	7
8	9	10	11	12	13	14
15	16	17	18	19	20	21
22	23	24	25	26	27	28
29	30	31				

FEBRUARY
S	M	T	W	T	F	S
			1	2	3	4
5	6	7	8	9	10	11
12	13	14	15	16	17	18
19	20	21	22	23	24	25
26	27	28	29			

MARCH
S	M	T	W	T	F	S
				1	2	3
4	5	6	7	8	9	10
11	12	13	14	15	16	17
18	19	20	21	22	23	24
25	26	27	28	29	30	31

APRIL
S	M	T	W	T	F
1	2	3	4	5	6
8	9	10	11	12	13
15	16	17	18	19	20
22	23	24	25	26	27
29	30				

MAY
S	M	T	W	T	F	S
		1	2	3	4	5
6	7	8	9	10	11	12
13	14	15	16	17	18	19
20	21	22	23	24	25	26
27	28	29	30	31		

JUNE
S	M	T	W	T	F	S
					1	2
3	4	5	6	7	8	9
10	11	12	13	14	15	16
17	18	19	20	21	22	23
24	25	26	27	28	29	30

JULY
S	M	T	W	T	F	S
1	2	3	4	5	6	7
8	9	10	11	12	13	14
15	16	17	18	19	20	21
22	23	24	25	26	27	28
29	30	31				

AUGUST
S	M	T	W	T	F
			1	2	3
5	6	7	8	9	10
12	13	14	15	16	17
19	20	21	22	23	24
26	27	28	29	30	31

SEPTEMBER
S	M	T	W	T	F	S
						1
2	3	4	5	6	7	8
9	10	11	12	13	14	15
16	17	18	19	20	21	22
23/30	24	25	26	27	28	29

OCTOBER
S	M	T	W	T	F	S
	1	2	3	4	5	6
7	8	9	10	11	12	13
14	15	16	17	18	19	20
21	22	23	24	25	26	27
28	29	30	31			

NOVEMBER
S	M	T	W	T	F	S
				1	2	3
4	5	6	7	8	9	10
11	12	13	14	15	16	17
18	19	20	21	22	23	24
25	26	27	28	29	30	

DECEMBER
S	M	T	W	T	F
2	3	4	5	6	7
9	10	11	12	13	14
16	17	18	19	20	21
23/30	24/31	25	26	27	28

1985

JANUARY
S	M	T	W	T	F	S
		1	2	3	4	5
6	7	8	9	10	11	12
13	14	15	16	17	18	19
20	21	22	23	24	25	26
27	28	29	30	31		

FEBRUARY
S	M	T	W	T	F	S
					1	2
3	4	5	6	7	8	9
10	11	12	13	14	15	16
17	18	19	20	21	22	23
24	25	26	27	28		

MARCH
S	M	T	W	T	F	S
					1	2
3	4	5	6	7	8	9
10	11	12	13	14	15	16
17	18	19	20	21	22	23
24/31	25	26	27	28	29	30

APRIL
S	M	T	W	T	F	S
	1	2	3	4	5	6
7	8	9	10	11	12	13
14	15	16	17	18	19	20
21	22	23	24	25	26	27
28	29	30				

MAY
S	M	T	W	T	F	S
			1	2	3	4
5	6	7	8	9	10	11
12	13	14	15	16	17	18
19	20	21	22	23	24	25
26	27	28	29	30	31	

JUNE
S	M	T	W	T	F	S
						1
2	3	4	5	6	7	8
9	10	11	12	13	14	15
16	17	18	19	20	21	22
23/30	24	25	26	27	28	29

JULY
S	M	T	W	T	F	S
	1	2	3	4	5	6
7	8	9	10	11	12	13
14	15	16	17	18	19	20
21	22	23	24	25	26	27
28	29	30	31			

AUGUST
S	M	T	W	T	F	S
				1	2	3
4	5	6	7	8	9	10
11	12	13	14	15	16	17
18	19	20	21	22	23	24
25	26	27	28	29	30	31

SEPTEMBER
S	M	T	W	T	F	S
1	2	3	4	5	6	7
8	9	10	11	12	13	14
15	16	17	18	19	20	21
22	23	24	25	26	27	28
29	30					

OCTOBER
S	M	T	W	T	F	S
		1	2	3	4	5
6	7	8	9	10	11	12
13	14	15	16	17	18	19
20	21	22	23	24	25	26
27	28	29	30	31		

NOVEMBER
S	M	T	W	T	F	S
					1	2
3	4	5	6	7	8	9
10	11	12	13	14	15	16
17	18	19	20	21	22	23
24	25	26	27	28	29	30

DECEMBER
S	M	T	W	T	F	S
1	2	3	4	5	6	7
8	9	10	11	12	13	14
15	16	17	18	19	20	21
22	23	24	25	26	27	28
29	30	31				

1986

JANUARY
S	M	T	W	T	F	S
			1	2	3	4
5	6	7	8	9	10	11
12	13	14	15	16	17	18
19	20	21	22	23	24	25
26	27	28	29	30	31	

FEBRUARY
S	M	T	W	T	F	S
						1
2	3	4	5	6	7	8
9	10	11	12	13	14	15
16	17	18	19	20	21	22
23	24	25	26	27	28	

MARCH
S	M	T	W	T	F	S
						1
2	3	4	5	6	7	8
9	10	11	12	13	14	15
16	17	18	19	20	21	22
23/30	24/31	25	26	27	28	29

APRIL
S	M	T	W	T	F	S
		1	2	3	4	5
6	7	8	9	10	11	12
13	14	15	16	17	18	19
20	21	22	23	24	25	26
27	28	29	30			

MAY
S	M	T	W	T	F	S
				1	2	3
4	5	6	7	8	9	10
11	12	13	14	15	16	17
18	19	20	21	22	23	24
25	26	27	28	29	30	31

JUNE
S	M	T	W	T	F	S
1	2	3	4	5	6	7
8	9	10	11	12	13	14
15	16	17	18	19	20	21
22	23	24	25	26	27	28
29	30					

JULY
S	M	T	W	T	F	S
		1	2	3	4	5
6	7	8	9	10	11	12
13	14	15	16	17	18	19
20	21	22	23	24	25	26
27	28	29	30	31		

AUGUST
S	M	T	W	T	F	S
					1	2
3	4	5	6	7	8	9
10	11	12	13	14	15	16
17	18	19	20	21	22	23
24/31	25	26	27	28	29	30

SEPTEMBER
S	M	T	W	T	F	S
	1	2	3	4	5	6
7	8	9	10	11	12	13
14	15	16	17	18	19	20
21	22	23	24	25	26	27
28	29	30				

OCTOBER
S	M	T	W	T	F	S
			1	2	3	4
5	6	7	8	9	10	11
12	13	14	15	16	17	18
19	20	21	22	23	24	25
26	27	28	29	30	31	

NOVEMBER
S	M	T	W	T	F	S
						1
2	3	4	5	6	7	8
9	10	11	12	13	14	15
16	17	18	19	20	21	22
23/30	24	25	26	27	28	29

DECEMBER
S	M	T	W	T	F	S
	1	2	3	4	5	6
7	8	9	10	11	12	13
14	15	16	17	18	19	20
21	22	23	24	25	26	27
28	29	30	31			